Motorbooks International

MIL-TECH SERIES

MIKOYAN
MiG-29

Design and Development of Russia's Super Fighter

Hans Halberstadt

To Olga, for everything

First published in 1992 by Motorbooks International Publishers & Wholesalers, PO Box 2, 729 Prospect Avenue, Osceola, WI 54020 USA

Motorbooks International books are also available at discounts in bulk quantity for industrial or sales-promotional use. For details write to Special Sales Manager at the Publisher's address

Library of Congress Cataloging-in-Publication Data
Halberstadt, Hans.
    Mikoyan MiG-29 / Hans Halberstadt.
      p.   cm.—(Motorbooks International mil-tech series)
    Includes index.
    ISBN 0-87938-656-8
    1. MiG-29 (Jet fighter plane)   I. Title.   II. Series.
UG1242.F5H32   1992
358.4'382—dc20   92-9011

On the front cover: A two-seat MiG-29UB from the Swifts flight demonstration team on short final at Kubinka air base, near Moscow.

On the back cover: Top, a MiG-29K makes an arrested landing aboard the Russian aircraft carrier *Kuznetzov. via John Lake*/World Air Power Journal. Center, a MiG-29A at Kubinka. Bottom, an overall view of the MiG-29's cockpit shows the excellent K-36D ejection seat.

Printed and bound in the United States of America

Contents

Acknowledgments

This book is the product of a cooperative effort by a great many Russians, in and out of government and the Air Force. It received generous support from the Mikoyan Design Bureau (OKB) and from the Air Force of the Moscow Military District. While it is intended to be a detailed portrait of a very famous airplane, it is a friendly picture, painted more from the Russian perspective than from the traditional Cold War Western view. We've heard a lot about the supposed faults and failures of Soviet weapons; this book is about systems that work and the people who designed them.

I'm particularly indebted to the small, new, extraordinary Russian company called AviaData—a group of former aerospace industry professionals who have gone private and now serve as a kind of public relations firm for Russian civilian and military aviation activities. The director of AviaData, Boris Rybak, did what everybody told me could not be done: He secured excellent cooperation from the then-Soviet Air Force and from the OKB where the MiG-29 came to life. I spent three weeks in Russia researching this project and, contrary to everything I'd heard, found the Russians businesslike, friendly, energetic, candid, and anxious to have their story told. AviaData delivered everything it promised—including an opportunity to fly in the aircraft. I had free run of an Air Force base for more than a week, with virtually no restrictions and usually no military escort.

I am indebted particularly to Mikhail Waldenberg, chief designer of the MiG-29; AviaData Director Rybak; Alexander Velovich, deputy director of AviaData; Anatoly Kvotchur, former test pilot for Mikoyan OKB; and the staff of AviaData. A special note of appreciation for their extraordinary support goes to both Lt. Gen. Nikolai Antoshkin, commander of the Air Force of the Moscow Military District, and Maj. Gen. Vladimir Sokolov, commander of the Air Division, with headquarters at Kubinka.

I also owe thanks to my wonderful hosts in Moscow, Nina and Leo Yakovlev, both retired from careers on the MiG-29 assembly line; they had never met an American before, spoke no English, and were—despite great misgivings—talked into hosting a visiting journalist from the capitalist-imperialist West. Of the many pleasures and privileges of my visit, I think I enjoyed the hospitality of this couple the most.

Preface

Until quite recently, a book about a major Soviet weapons system, such as the MiG-29, would have been about three pages long, two of which were blank and the other not filled with very much information. The Soviet Union wasn't telling or showing anything to anybody. Then, as a result of new attitudes and policies, Soviet

A MiG-29 poses for the camera somewhere high above the snowy Russian landscape.
AviaData

society began to open up, to itself and to the rest of the world. While Mikhail Gorbachov gets most of the credit for the change—and properly so—he was part of a process, not its inventor. The changes were inevitable, but he formalized the beginning of the process. And as soon as the door was opened, it was opened all the way.

That process is important if you admire airplanes, because the Soviets are among the most imaginative and creative artists in the medium of aircraft design. Their design bureaus (OKBs)—Ilyushin, Yakovlev, Mikoyan, Tupolev, and others— have been turning out some of the fastest, largest, most powerful, agile, capable, and, sometimes, curious fighters, helicopters, transports, and sport aircraft anywhere.

Until just a few years ago, when the policy of "openness" began, these designs were visible only in grainy, out-of-focus illustrations in *Jane's All the World's Aircraft*. That, happily, is no longer the case.

This book is a product of the new attitude in Moscow, the result of a long look at operational fighters, not demonstration aircraft, and at an operational air base in Russia. It is also the result of long and detailed interviews with the MiG-29's senior designer, Mikhail Waldenberg, and one of the USSR's most honored and famous test pilots, Anatoly Kvotchur, in Moscow. Air Force pilots also contributed their insights and observations. And, a major contribution was made by a small, private Russian company, AviaData, which made the arrangements for the

The gate to Kubinka Air Base. Security is surprisingly light; guards are much more casual than at American bases—and don't carry guns.

visits to Kubinka Air Base and the interviews with designers, pilots, and staff, and provided much of the support necessary to tell the story. The AviaData staff are all former employees of the aircraft OKBs, and several worked on systems used on the MiG-29.

As a product of the Cold War years, I found going into the Soviet Union an intimidating experience. I grew up thinking that the USSR was the enemy, that a significant threat of nuclear war existed, and believed until very recently that the Soviets were intent on global domination. I've been shot at with Soviet-designed weapons, and I've shot at people professing Soviet-style politics. So, I was a bit apprehensive about how these people would react, what they would say, how they would say it.

What they said was, "Photograph anything you want, ask any question." I was offered a ride in the aircraft. They brought out a rack of live missiles for me to inspect and photograph in detail. I was encouraged to photograph cockpits of operational aircraft. Only a couple of years before, any of this would have been enough to get me shot (and not with a camera, either). In fact, the access was even more complete, less restrictive, and friendlier than that I get at American bases sometimes. When I asked why, they said, "We want people in the West to understand us as we really are. Tell the truth about us and the aircraft, in detail. That will be enough."

The research was done at Kubinka Air Base, near Moscow. Kubinka is sometimes called a show base because it is occasionally used to host visitors and for demonstrations. But away from the small exhibition area, it is a very average Soviet air base and extremely different from its

One of the many Russian pilots who helped in the production of this book, getting settled before slipping the surly bonds of Earth.

Western counterparts. Out on the long flight line are aircraft of many kinds: fighters, transports, helicopters, ground attack and liaison planes. There was a glittering Il-76 transport and an antique An-2 biplane, still used by the Soviets. The MiGs were parked in dispersal areas that suggested wartime security measures rather than a demonstration and exhibition facility. As far as I could tell (and I was looking for it), there was no effort to provide special aircraft for my benefit.

Business went on as usual, without a ripple. For military people new to the mission of what we call "public affairs," the Soviets did a marvelous job. But they have something good to show off in the MiG-29, something they're proud of—and rightfully so. They said they wished the airplane had a good Russian name, but they call it the Fulcrum, just as we do. Here, then, is the MiG-29 Fulcrum air superiority fighter.

By 1988 the Fulcrum was showing up on magazine covers, including Aviation and Cosmonautics, *one of the many periodicals published by the Soviet Air Force. The pilots shown are wearing high-altitude pressure suits, not the regular helmet and flight suit used for conventional missions.* Jon Lake/ World Air Power Journal

One of the early MiG-29 prototypes attracts a crowd at the aviation museum just off Leningradski Prospect near downtown Moscow. The founders of the OKB, Mikoyan and Gurevich, are in the large photograph in the front of the aircraft.

Chapter 1

A Russian War Story

The scenario: Far away, over the horizon, flashes of summer lightning punctuate the night. A sound like distant thunder—a flat, muted rumble—carries across the miles. The flashes come from the clouds, but not in the natural way; they are from bombs delivered by medium and heavy bombers. The bombs are falling on air bases, communications facilities, railroad bridges, and highways. Across a vast front, hundreds of tactical and strategic aircraft strike targets with direct and indirect military importance. The attack is well planned, carefully coordinated, devastatingly effective—and a surprise.

Even so, missile batteries and air defense artillery units go into action and begin firing. Some of the flashes are visible now in the predawn sky: a quick explosion in the darkness, and then a trail of fire falling to the ground.

The big missiles, the ones most able to hit the invading flights, are part of massive batteries that rely on separate radars for detection and targeting and on a complex, highly integrated command-and-control network for employment. But as the powerful radars are turned on, they instantly become visible to the invading forces' electronic warfare specialists. The radar energy becomes a beacon for the attackers, pinpointing important targets. Antiradiation missiles slide off the rails of special planes in every invading flight, planes whose sole mission is to blind the defenders. One after another, the huge radars are engulfed by fire and blast effect and are effectively converted to scrap metal. The surface-to-air missiles they were intended to serve remain silent on their launch rails, impotently aimed at the sky. Without the radars, they can't be guided to the targets overhead.

Many of the radars do survive by being used carefully and cautiously. The operators turn them on for just a few seconds at a time—enough for a quick peek—and shut them down long before an antiradiation missile can be effectively launched at them. But the invading force has other ways to counter the defenses, among them electronic warfare. The electronic warfare aircraft are few in number and odd in appearance, with aerials and antennas and pods sprouting from wings and fuselages. They orbit well away from the actual target areas and, instead of rockets or missiles, fire invisible electrical energy in the carefully crafted form of radio waves. Inside the command centers on the ground, where commanders and technicians are desperately trying to find the pattern of the attack and to direct forces to defend against it, the voice and data links dissolve into noise and static. The defense is now becoming mute as well as blind.

Still, the attack is opposed, if even in an uncoordinated way. There are enough resources and alternatives that the battle is costly for both the attacker and the defender. As the sun rises on the first day of the war, across a wide and deep battlefield, the forces of the Soviet Union and the Warsaw Pact are fully engaged in combat with the invading armies and air forces of the North Atlantic Treaty Organization (NATO).

Despite a reputation for tight control, the doctrine of the Warsaw Pact anticipates just the kind of confusion and isolation and losses that this most recent of invasions has imposed. So, without orders or direction, tank units and fighter squadrons are prepared for battle and are pointed toward the distant sound of guns. On the ground, tank regiment commanders and their staffs improvise hasty defenses, engage the lead elements of the assault, destroy some, and then withdraw to new positions. Both the attackers and defenders suffer attrition, but the defenders gain time, while the attackers lose it.

In the air over the battlefield swarm close air support fighters and attack helicopters, just above the trees, just ahead of the lead elements, and scouting off on the flanks. They are incredibly successful in the initial hours as defenders, and attackers make contact, but the sheer number and variety of air defense weapons—guns of large and small calibers, short-range, heat-seeking missiles, plus counter-

A Russian fighter pilot, Major Alexander Datalov. Men like this—highly trained, well informed about NATO aircraft and tactics, motivated, and supplied with excellent weapons—would make the cost high for any future invader of Russia.

air electronic warfare systems—take a toll of the A-10s and helicopters trying to cover the NATO armor spearheads.

Although the NATO bombers quickly damage or destroy the air bases in range of the battlefield, very few aircraft are destroyed on the ground. The bases are virtually empty. A few days before the invasion, as tensions escalated, the Air Force command ordered the air regiments, obvious targets in the event of war, to leave their bases.

A pilot and crew chief inspect an aircraft before flight. The crew chief is a commissioned officer, probably a lieutenant—unlike his Western counterpart, who would be a noncommissioned officer, a sergeant. His hand rests on the leading edge of the port stabilator, a massive control surface that is one factor in the fighter's tremendous low-speed agility. Above the pilot's head is one of several air data sensors. The top of the fin incorporates an antenna (inside the tip), a navigation light, and a radar-warning system receiver. This aircraft is an early model without the chaff and flare dispensers that were added to aircraft built after combat experience in Afghanistan. AviaData

A pair of Fulcrums turn to port, both with nearly empty racks and rails. Normal combat load includes six AA-10A long-range radar-guided missiles and/or AA-11 infrared missiles for shorter ranges. AviaData

The Soviets long ago learned the hazards of relying on established and elaborate bases for their airplanes during war. Not only are such bases easily targeted, but they are seldom convenient to the battle. They also learned the need for good combat aviation the hard way during World War II, at a cost of 25 million lives—a lesson not easily forgotten.

So, in hundreds of places across Eastern Europe a few aircraft could be found incongruously operating from dirt roads, highways, and roughly prepared cow pastures. Instead of big hangars and elaborate facilities, the fighter aircraft are attended by two or three trucks and a dozen maintenance personnel. One truck provides fuel and another is loaded with bombs, rockets, and missiles. The conditions are primitive, but the fighters have returned from one mission against the attacking forces and are quickly being readied for another.

There's a straight stretch of dirt road only 100km from the "forward edge of battle area" (FEBA), and it has been taken over by a pair of MiG-29s and their tiny collection of attendant trucks and troops. They've just returned from their first combat, part of a hastily planned saturation attack against the NATO airborne early-warning aircraft that give the invasion force's airplanes their long-range eyes and ears. Even though the armored assault is pressing quickly into Soviet territory, the priority target now is the AWACS planes

The old Soviet Air Force patch, so proudly worn for many years, has become a collector's item.

and their airborne warning and control systems. The AWACS are heavily defended and far to the rear, but they must be removed at whatever cost.

The pair of MiGs will be airborne at 1000 hours and will participate in a massive, coordinated, dangerous mission aimed at the AWACS. Even though there are just a few of them, each will be able to see every attacking plane and will be able to help coordinate its own defense. The actual engagement of the AWACS will probably fall to Su-27 interceptors, with the MiG-29 fighters engaging the F-15s that provide cover for the lumbering giants.

While the two pilots stand by the side of the road, the ground crews swarm around and on top of the MiGs, sliding fresh missiles on the rails beneath the wings, pumping fuel into the tanks, rearming 30mm cannons, and inspecting for damage. The pilots don't take any of their flight gear off, but smoke a quick cigarette and talk and gesture excitedly. The thunder of guns and bombs is audible in the distance, and the very ground seems to tremble. The crew chief, a lieutenant, runs over; the jets are ready.

Each pilot climbs a ladder and remounts his fighter. The crew chief helps the pilot adjust his ejection seat harness, then climbs down the ladder and removes it. After a quick check of switch positions and a glance over at his wingman, the pilot moves the engine ignition switch to START, advances the throttle to IDLE, and watches the gauges as the turbine engine starts to spin. The engine begins a gentle hum as the compressor blades turn and bite the air—a single, rising tone. Fuel is automatically injected into the combustion chamber of the Number One engine and, in a sudden burst of power, the MiG surges forward as the engine comes alive with a roar. In the cockpit, the pilot watches the instruments: rpm rising smoothly and steadily, exhaust gas temperature coming up and stabilizing in the green, and fuel flow, hydraulic pressure, and generator output all normal and in the green. The second engine lights off and comes up to speed the same way. The canopy comes down. A glance at the wingman reveals that he's ready, too, and, so, with a quick nod of his head, the flight leader indicates he's ready for takeoff.

Back from a mission, two MiG pilots debrief. The one on the right is Colonel Alexander Kutuzov, deputy commander of the Kubinka air regiment. He wears the new Russian flight suit over his "speed jeans" and a heavy winter flying jacket over that. The new version of the flight suit incorporates a map pocket with a transparent window in the right leg. The pilot on the left keeps his comfortable helmet on, as many of his comrades do; Russian flight gear is light, comfortable, and efficient.

There is no tower to call, no permission to request. The MiG is already lined up on the road/runway, so the pilot just stands on the brakes, slides the throttle smoothly forward into afterburner, and then releases the brakes to start the takeoff roll. The dirt road is uneven and the nose wheel kicks up rocks and dirt, but the MiG is designed to cope. In any other nation's aircraft, the rocks would end up in the engine air intakes and would invariably be ingested by the engine, but not on a MiG. The sleek fighter was built to fly and fight from primitive strips like this one, so the main engine air inlets are covered during takeoff and landing. While the main inlets are closed, the engines breathe air through alternate intakes on top of the wing roots, protected from flying rocks and mud; when the plane is airborne and airspeed is sufficient, the main intakes will open.

Even with a full combat load of AA-11 and AA-10 missiles and a full 150 rounds of 30mm cannon shells, the MiG leaps into the air after a short takeoff roll. As soon as the dust settles enough, the Number Two aircraft lines up on the road, applies power, and launches itself into the air.

The displays on the AWACS aircraft start to show numerous "bogies," enemy planes materializing from the ground clutter beyond the FEBA—from places far from any airfield. The technicians try to track the swarm, but there are too many. Even so, the NATO fighters providing air cover hear the AWACS crew call bearings and ranges. The voices on the NATO net rise in pitch and the speech is a little faster as the adrenaline flows. The big AWACS radar can see all for hundreds of miles, but it, like any other radar, becomes a beacon for anyone bold enough to try to find it. The screens on the big plane show hundreds of defenders rising from the landscape, a swarm whose purpose soon becomes all too obvious. Desperately, F-15s,

F-16s, Tornados, and Mirages are vectored from primary missions to defend against the sudden threat. On the AWACS screens, the symbologies for friendly and enemy forces merge into tangled masses from which one symbol or another emerges. Often, the technicians see a MiG or Sukhoi disappear from the screen, victims of Sidewinder or Sparrow missiles. But there are so many bogies that the fighters covering the NATO attack are momentarily overwhelmed—sheer numbers of the Soviet planes saturating the defenses and permitting some MiGs and Sukhois to muscle past the Eagles and Falcons at speeds exceeding that of sound, more than 800mph. Their objective is all too horribly clear to the AWACS crew.

The big plane turns away from the battlefield, and dozens of fighters converge to screen it from the enemy. One by one, the NATO aircraft are engaged and fight for their lives—sometimes successfully, sometimes not. Inevitably, as was the Soviet battle plan, some MiGs and Su-27s get past the defenders and into missile range. The Sukhois begin launching their AA-10 missiles at distances beyond the ranges at which they are supposed to be effective, more than forty miles from the AWACS. The inbound missiles are tracked by the AWACS, and the big aircraft's F-15 and F-16 defenders' countermeasures systems start punching out chaff and flares.

Out in the "fur-ball," a MiG flight of two hunts for F-15s to engage, and finds them. The Eagles are tremendously fast and agile, with superb weapons and fire-control systems. They have great track-while-scan radar linked to a highly advanced fire-control system far more sophisticated than that on the MiG. They are low, hiding in the ground clutter, hoping for a shot at an unwary MiG or Sukhoi, closing at more than 800mph with the approaching Soviet aircraft. They launch long-range Sparrow radar-guided missiles and continue to close; the MiGs and Su-27s spot the missiles immediately and evade. At the same time, they start dispensing chaff to counter the radar missile threat. Several of the missiles detonate against clouds of aluminum foil; another turns a Soviet aircraft into aluminum scrap.

Russian ground control intercept stations have been tracking the flights with a radar net too large to destroy in one attack. The radar stations are connected with fiber-optic cable land lines, with digital data links over microwave transmission nets and over radios with jam-resistant, frequency-hopping systems. The controllers plot the invading flights and provide vectors to the interceptors and fighters. The attackers have extensive electronic warfare assets: large airborne jamming platforms, sophisticated systems to counter the Russian command-and-control net. They work against some of the radio communications systems, but not all, and not enough.

Using digital data-burst transmissions, the controllers are able to give the interceptors enough information to stop the attacking flights.

The opposing fighters converge, too close for the Sparrows. In the F-15 cockpits, pilots squirm in their seats, trying to find the bogies. The ones in front show on radar, but the radar-warning receivers are silent. The bogies are not using radar and,

The infrared search-and-track (IRST) ball incorporates a mirror in a glass sphere that rotates to view a large portion of the forward hemisphere. This passive sensor is the key to the MiGs' "Stealthy" capability; it is slaved to a powerful laser rangefinder.

A rack of AA-11 missiles—genuine "war shots" and not inert training rounds.

consequently, are not advertising their positions.

One MiG pilot racks his airplane into hard turns just above the deck, watching the multifunction display on his head up display, glancing occasionally at the weapons system screen on the right side of the instrument panel. A target appears, tracked by the infrared (IR) seeker, at three o'clock and a range of 30km. The pilot designates the target, which is not squawking a friendly identification-friend-or-foe (IFF) code, and launches an AA-10 missile. It misses, spoofed by a cloud of chaff, and explodes near the Eagle, but not near enough.

The MiG turns hard right. The Eagle turns to the attacker, closing fast. In seconds, they are in heat-seeking missile range, and both launch and squirm to evade and attack.

But the MiG has some sophistication of its own. The Eagle depends on radar for detection and guidance; the MiG also uses radar, but has a better system for this kind of fighting. The MiG's fire-control system is based on an IR seeker/tracker (IRST) that uses the target's heat signature as a primary detection system. When an aircraft like the F-15 uses its radar, it broadcasts its position and its intentions to the world; that's why every combat aircraft has a radar-warning receiver that indicates bearing and sometimes the range to a hostile system. The MiG's IRST system is passive. It offers no warning.

Two MiGs with a ground attack mission roll in on an enemy logistics support column of trucks and vans, the essential "beans and bullets" that sustain the attack. They spot the column at a distance of several miles—out of effective range of the invaders' air defense weapons, but close enough to be seen.

Each MiG carries six rocket launcher pods on pylons beneath their wings, thirty-two 57mm rockets in each. The rockets would be useless against the thick frontal armor of a tank but are highly effective on the thinner skins of the vehicles. The fighters come in at treetop level, using the terrain for protection, and then pop up, roll inverted, and fire.

The armored column, alert to air attack, defends with IR missiles, main guns, automatic weapons, and air defense systems. The fighters' countermeasures systems automatically eject chaff and flares to spoof the radar and thermal sensors of the target's defensive systems, decoying missiles and confusing the air defense artillery radar.

Exposed for only seconds, both jets launch 128 rockets each in ripple fire, with programmed delays between firings of microseconds. The result is a target area saturated with fire. Rockets connect with vehicles, near-misses spray troops and trucks with shrapnel, and the convoy ceases to exist.

High overhead, a pair of F-16s close in on bogies that happen to be MiG-29s. The invaders suspect enemy aircraft but are reluctant to fire because of the numerous friendly fighters in the vicinity. They continue to close, attempting to make visual identification—a fatal mistake. Within seconds, the two flights are too close for radar missiles, and they break up into one-on-one sparring matches with IR missiles and guns.

Falcon pilots launch Sidewinder IR missiles at MiG-29 Fulcrums; some of them connect, but others are spoofed by flares. Fulcrum pilots launch Archer IR missiles at F-16s; again, some connect and others are decoyed. Both types of aircraft can turn tightly, and 9g turns are sustained for long seconds, pilots fighting to retain consciousness and to gain position.

One of the Falcons finds a Fulcrum in range but out of position to be able to lock on with his Sidewinder missile. The turning, pitching, scissoring game of wits evolves, and the airspeed of both fighters decays from 500 to 400 to 300 to 200 knots and then goes back up again. The Fulcrum dives away, turning and popping chaff and flares; the Falcon follows, getting lock-on tone intermittently. Diving almost vertically, his plane's airspeed accelerates rapidly for a moment, and the Falcon pilot can see the MiG-29 afterburner's long tongues of flame suddenly go out as the fighter pitches upward. Still in afterburner, the F-16 closes for the kill—but shoots right past the Fulcrum, suspended

Colonel Alexander Kutuzov would be responsible for much of the tactical employment of the air wing if and when the Russian Air Force goes to war again. He and the other pilots at Kubinka have to worry about the very real possibility of war among the republics that once formed the Soviet Union.

in a nearly motionless hover. The tables are suddenly turned; to his horror, the Falcon pilot sees over his shoulder the Fulcrum at his "six" and the flash of the AA-11 Archer IR missile as it launches. In seconds, the missile impacts, the F-16 starts to crumble, and the pilot braces himself and punches out.

A pair of Fulcrums 100km away close on a KC-10 tanker, the "fuel station in the sky" for the invasion fleet. The tanker is, of course, protected by several fighters, but the tactics of the Russian squadrons anticipated that. By sending a whole squadron at the target, from many directions and altitudes, the defense should quickly become saturated. And that's how it happens. The pair, Hawk Six and Hawk Seven, are vectored to the target, sweeping in at treetop height, and then pull up beneath the KC-10. One of the defending F-15 Eagles engages in a slashing, head-on attack. The MiGs are forced to maneuver, but Hawk Seven gets within 2km; with the tanker target visible off to the aircraft's left, the pilot watches it for two seconds and, by using his helmet-mounted sight, designates the target for his AA-11 missile. The Archer leaps from its rail and swoops away from the MiG in a high, squirming turn; another AA-11 follows after a moment, just to be sure. The first missile ignores the flares launched by the target and hits the Number Two engine; a fireball 400m across blooms astern of the MiG, and the second AA-11 explodes uselessly in it as the attackers turn away, engaged by the F-16s.

Across the skies of Eastern Europe, the airborne battle rages. At stake is control of the air; without it, control of the ground is impossible. In the hundreds of brittle skirmishes, victory sometimes goes to the invader and sometimes to the defender. But in the end and at great cost, the invasion slows and finally stops and turns away—defeated by a huge "com-

18

bined arms" army—and another chapter is written of the long history of Russia turning back invaders.

This preceding scenario is, of course, pure fiction, and Soviet fiction at that. As unlikely as it may seem to us in the West, there was a real fear by many, at all levels of Soviet society, of a NATO-initiated war with the Warsaw Pact. Luckily, despite four decades of tension and conflict, the forces of NATO and the Warsaw Pact never engaged in actual direct combat. And now, the Soviet Union is itself gone, replaced by the Commonwealth of Independent States.

But this scenario certainly does represent what Soviet planners *thought* could have happened; it reflected one contingency of many and what the Warsaw Pact planned for in the event of a shooting conflict with NATO forces. Many billions of dollars, rubles, pounds, Deutchemarks, and lira were invested in preparing for World War III. And while the idea of an invasion of the Soviet Union and the other members of the Warsaw Pact might seem ridiculous to us, it certainly seemed plausible to the Russians. And with many good reasons; they've been invaded and threatened with invasion for centuries.

Weapons systems such as the ones on the MiG-29 are only small components of massive, complicated, and expensive strategic plans for things that *might* happen. The MiG-29 is one extension of the commitment of the Soviet Union to be able to fight any adversary in the future, because they have had to deal with so many adversaries in the past. Russian history—and that of the other republics, as well—is dominated by a recurrent theme of invasions by the Germans, French, Swedes, and Asians, and wars with all possible neighbors. Russian history is full of military disaster and economic victimization. The Mongol hordes rampaged through early Russia, and Nazi Germans did the same just a few decades ago. While the United States and the Soviet Union were both victims of surprise attacks at the outset of World War II, we lost half a million men in battle, but the Soviets lost 27 million men, women, and children to combat and starvation and disease. The experience was just another chapter in their history, nothing really new. But World War II's awful cost inspired Soviet society to ensure that the next invasion would be met with an unbeatable military establishment.

The Soviets learned many lessons during what they call the "Great Patriotic War," the most important of which was to prepare for worst-case scenarios. Another is that a lot of good weapons systems are better than a few excellent weapons systems, and that battles may be won by good defense, but wars are won by good attacks. The Soviets have incorporated all these lessons in their combat aircraft, particularly the marvelous MiG-29.

Now that the Soviet Union is gone and the paranoia of the Cold War with it, the peoples of Russia, Ukraine, Georgia, and all the other independent republics of the Commonwealth still feel threatened. When I visited Kubinka in October 1991, several MiG-29 pilots made the point of saying that they were not worried about any threat from the West—but they were sincerely worried about having to fight forces from breakaway republics as established order deteriorated. The threat of war among the republics is real, and the MiG pilots know that they're a first line of defense in any kind of skirmish. So, even with the threat of war with NATO gone, the MiG still has a role to play, a mission to perform.

The MiG-29 is an "air superiority" fighter aircraft, which means that its principal mission is to control the skies within its combat radius. According to the Mikoyan Design Bureau (OKB), its basic missions include "counter-air" or fighter versus fighter engagements, close air support, and counter-air reconnaissance, day or night, in any weather.

The Fulcrum is equipped for a day-only, clear-weather close air support role, but it has extremely accurate systems for delivering weapons against point targets (such as a tank or a bridge) or area targets (typically, troops in the open).

It has the systems to effectively engage other fighters at long, intermediate, and close ranges, and includes a fire-control system that gives a trained and motivated pilot some tactical advantages not available to fighters from other nations.

It carries a look-down, shoot-down radar that can pick targets out from the ground clutter. It has a digital data link that provides secure, reliable communications with ground command-and-control facilities. It carries an integrated fire-control system that automates separate weapons systems and targeting devices. Its weapons systems are known to be extremely effective; the cannon-and-laser-rangefinder system is said to guarantee a kill on any target in range with no more than five rounds.

The MiG-29 airframe-powerplant combination was intended to be superior to any other contemporary fighter; it has a thrust-to-weight ratio of better than 1:1, which means that it can accelerate while

MiG-29 on a very short final for Kubinka's one long runway.

flying straight up while carrying a normal combat load. And it can pull 9gs and more, for as long as the pilot can stand it. The airframe will take 12gs without bending, even though no pilot can do the same.

The plane is agile in ways that only counter-air combat aircraft need to be: You can control it easily when it's going very fast or very slow, up or down, straight and level or squirming in a gun fight. It can perform combat maneuvers that Western fighters can't duplicate, and is considered by some Western experts to be superior in important ways to anything else in the air.

It is intended to be able to identify, engage, and defeat any contemporary fighter or bomber—and it probably can, often without being detected itself. It is a simple, strong, elegant, and sophisticated combat aircraft, intended to be easy to maintain under the most austere conditions and with the most minimal of facilities. It doesn't need a runway or a hangar; a dirt road will serve for landings and all maintenance is done in the open air.

The MiG's fire-control system, with its IRST system, powerful look-down shoot-down radar, laser rangefinder, extremely accurate 30mm cannon, and helmet-mounted sight, are all integrated into a package that is extremely effective and unique. The MiG-29 can carry three kinds of missiles, all state-of-the-art, and it can carry them at better than Mach 2, around 1500mph.

Like many Soviet weapons systems, the MiG has been slandered and belittled by Western media reports—until the re-

Turning to final, gear down, flaps down, leading edge extensions out, a MiG-29 Fulcrum comes back to the roost. AviaData

porters got a good look at it. Until the MiG-29 visited Finland, it was criticized for a variety of imagined flaws and faults. Since then, many Western military and aerospace industry experts have been able to see the MiG perform, and what they have seen is a set of capabilities unmatched by any combat aircraft in any air force.

Although the Fulcrum (as NATO calls it) appeared earlier, the 1988 visit to the Farnborough Air Show in Great Britain was the first real opportunity Western aviation analysts had to see the mystery fighter up close and doing its stuff. The reaction was one of surprise, for several reasons. One of the reasons was the candor of the Soviet pilots and technical experts who accompanied the aircraft, offering a wealth of detail about the fighter's systems and capabilities that had previously been classified state secrets. Not only was the technical information surprising, but the Soviets themselves surprised the journalists and military analysts with their charm and goodwill. After four decades of adversarial relations, the visit and the visitors did a lot to start a process of improving relations between the NATO forces and those of the Warsaw Pact. But the real thrill came when the MiGs flew what one aviation magazine called a "stunning" display.

When the two aircraft visited Farnborough in 1988, it was an unprecedented opportunity to study an aircraft that had been, until then, a major mystery. The visit began as the flight entered British airspace: a pair of Tornados formed up alongside to provide escort service. Waiting on the ground were crowds of aviation enthusiasts from many nations and many specialized interests, including a major intelligence-gathering effort by British and American teams using airborne and ground data collection devices. Every second the aircraft were aloft was recorded on videotape and thousands of photographs were taken. And, when the airplanes were safely parked and the pilots were formally greeted, interviewers for news magazines, radio, television—and the military intelligence community—interrogated the pilots and support personnel.

The planes were flown by Anatoly Kvotchur and Roman Taskaev, both highly accomplished test pilots from Mikoyan; Yuri Ermakov navigated. Accompanying them in an Aeroflot transport were a team from Mikoyan OKB, including Chief Designer Mikhail Waldenberg and Alexander Velovich, an avionics designer providing translation services.

The Russians surprised the crowd with their charm, candor, and, especially, their aerial display. It began with a full-burner takeoff, the MiG becoming airborne in only 750ft. That impressed the crowd, but what really shocked many of them was that the engine inlet doors stayed solidly closed during the entire run.

As soon as the wheels left the concrete, the nose of the jet was smoothly rotated straight up, and the MiG accelerated in a vertical climb and then continued to pull back into a loop that topped out at about 2,400ft. At the bottom of the loop, the MiG was started right back up again, but this time the power was chopped and the airspeed decayed until the fighter hung motionless in the air before sliding backward for a short distance. The pilot applied power at this point, pushed the nose back toward the horizon where it normally belongs, and—still completely in control—brought it back for more. This time, the MiG made a pass at low speed, only 110 knots, and extreme angle-of-attack (alpha), about twenty-five units of alpha, still in complete control. Then, the Fulcrum accelerated, pulled up to the vertical, and came back for another go, this time with the wings held vertical in a "knife-edge" pass. During the knife-edge maneuver, the aircraft was accelerated from about 270 knots to more than 450 knots. This was followed by a series of Cuban Eights and extreme turns, and then a roll into the landing pattern. While inverted, the gear were extended, and while still airborne (just a few feet above the ground) the braking parachute was deployed with a loud pop, and the MiG-29 was back on terra firma.

This display shot down a lot of notions about Soviet aircraft and airmen. The tailslide maneuver showed that the fighter was extraordinarily controllable under the most extreme of flight conditions and that the engines were far more capable than expected—and in the resistance to stall in the slide perhaps were superior to those of any manufacturer. After years of being disparaged by the Western media, the MiG was revealed to be an aircraft with performance equal to or better than anything else in the air. It did things no NATO fighter would attempt near the ground, if at all. It appeared to be controllable and agile both at high speeds and while hovering almost motionless in the air. In addition, the aircraft was simple (or at least as simple as a contemporary fighter can be), reliable, and designed to be operated from austere facilities when required.

The MiG-29 is certainly one of the most important fighter aircraft currently available. But like its contemporaries, whose designs came off the drawing boards in the 1960s and 1970s, the MiG-29 has its limitations and restrictions. Even its designers say its cockpit is crowded and complicated and makes the pilot's combat workload heavier than newer designs. Its flight control system uses hydraulics and mechanical linkages rather than the newer digital fly-by-wire technologies that help make such fighters as the F-15E Strike Eagle so much more agile. The airframe has limitations and flaws, like any aircraft's. But, as Canadian Air Force pilot Major Bob Wade said after flying it, "The Western pilot would be wise to detect and shoot at the MiG-29 from a distance using his high-technology weapons system, because if it comes down to a close encounter with infrared missiles or guns, a good Soviet pilot is a definite threat." (*Aviation Week*, February 26, 1990)

Chapter 2

Mikoyan Design Bureau

The MiG-29 is the product of an aerospace company and industry that is similar in many ways to those of Western nations. The name "MiG" is certainly the most famous of several major Soviet Design Bureaus (OKBs). It is actually an acronym for the abbreviated names of the two founders, Artyom Mikoyan and Mikhail Gurevich, who began working in the aircraft industry during the 1930s and established their own shop in 1939. In the late 1940s and throughout the 1950s, the Mikoyan OKB turned out many famous fighters before the MiG-29: the MiG-15, MiG-19, MiG-21, and MiG-25.

Rather like such Western companies as McDonnell Douglas, Mikoyan worked closely with the government yet stayed independent of it. Consequently, some of the MiG designs were the direct result of requests from the Soviet government to meet a set of given requirements, while others began as "free-lance" ideas, pure speculations about what might be needed in the future. The Fulcrum began life as a gleam in a designer's eye about 1970, but it had plenty of company at that stage. In 1972, the rough outline of the concept looked good enough to be formalized in a "technical assignment."

The Mikoyan OKB is in a large office building on Leningradski Prospect, just a fifteen-minute ride on the Metro "Green Line" from the Kremlin. Mikoyan OKB is one of several bureaus in the immediate neighborhood of the Moscow Aviation Institute, the school that produces most of the designers for the Soviet aviation industry. Next door is the Yakovlev OKB, where the Yak-38 Forger attack aircraft was designed. Across the street, Ilyushin OKB is busy working on big transports, including the successful Il-76 Candid.

These bureaus are a lot like American or British aerospace firms, competing for projects, speculating on the future needs of the industry, carving specialized niches in aerospace design.

The design process began gradually in the late 1960s in response to changes in NATO tactics and aircraft. During the 1950s and 1960s, before the development of really effective surface-to-air missiles (SAMs), NATO forces anticipated high-altitude engagements, with massive formations of strategic bombers and fighter escorts penetrating Warsaw Pact airspace. The general military aviation community did not take seriously the Soviet development of SAMs until a U-2 reconnaissance aircraft piloted by Francis Gary Powers was blown out of the high-altitude sky over the USSR in 1960. So much for the high-altitude penetration idea.

Consequently, low-altitude, dual-role fighters like the F-111 started appearing, designed to sneak under the Soviet radar and SAM defenses. Airborne radars of the period were designed to deal with high-altitude bogies; a low-altitude target could hide against the ground clutter. The terrific interceptors and fighters the Soviets

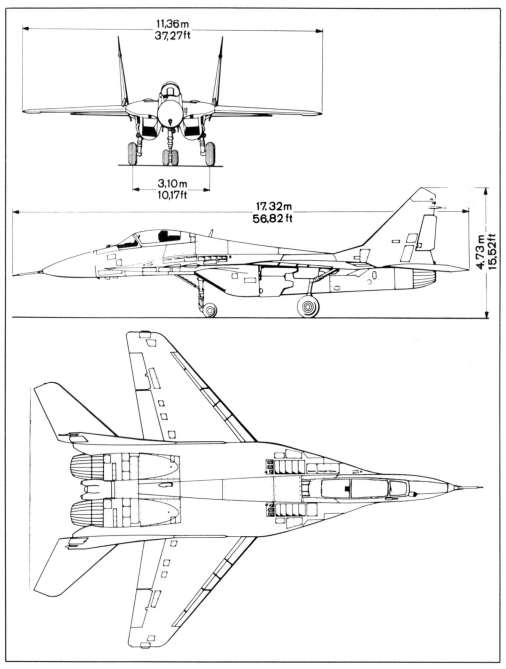

Plan and elevation drawings from Mikoyan
Design Bureau. AviaData

had been turning out, such as the MiG-25 Foxbat with its near-Mach 3 speed, suddenly became obsolete. Why? They had the agility of a moose, their radar was useless against low targets, and the pilot couldn't see a target unless it was conveniently straight ahead. Their combat tactics were based on the notion that ground control intercept (GCI) facilities would be able to effectively control the defense of the airspace by radio commands to the airborne fighters and interceptors. The new Western fighters, and their electronic warfare capability, meant that Russia and her allies were once again threatened.

What was needed to deal with these new threats was something like them, only better, with Doppler look-down, shoot-down radar, and long-range, be-yond-visual-range (BVR), radar-guided missiles to match. Also needed were heat-seekers and guns for the inevitable close encounters and the ability to turn hard, fly slowly, and still point the nose and the gun.

In about 1970, the designers started plotting and scheming and, as designers do everywhere, came up with dozens of possibilities. The designs evolved into models for wind tunnel tests. The Air Force got involved early and often. In 1972, the process stopped being a strictly speculative venture by Mikoyan and became formalized as a requirement, with funding and a schedule. The specifications meant that the new aircraft would need new kinds of engines, avionics, construction materials and techniques, and, especially, a new kind of shape.

The Mikoyan Design Bureau trademark on a MiG-29 demonstration aircraft.

One of the Mikoyan designers was Mikhail Waldenberg, the chief designer for the MiG-29. He is a charming man of great energy and good humor, about sixty years old, and has worked on the MiG-15, MiG-17, MiG-19, MiG-21, MiG-25, and MiG-29. He, former Mikoyan test pilot Anatoly Kvotchur, and avionics designer Alexander Velovich agreed to be interviewed for this book. All have been asked many questions about the MiG during the last few years, and it's obvious they're extremely proud and enthusiastic about the aircraft. The interviews were all conducted at the apartment where I was staying in Moscow, just down the road from the Mikoyan OKB, over several evenings. I asked them to talk about the aircraft's vices and virtues, to compare it to Western aircraft, and to discuss the Russian perspective on fighter development.

Mikhail Waldenberg:

I have been chief designer from 1982 to the present, including the flight test program, the actual production of the design, its introduction into service, and the program of modifications that is still continuing.

Who was responsible for the design of the aircraft? It was not a single person, but the product of its time. The basic design decisions belong to our general designer, Belyakov, who, being the head of the company, acted in many respects as chief designer of the MiG-29 since its early design stages. The design was the product of Mikoyan OKB, with contributions from several scientific research organizations: TzAgi [the Central Aero/ Hydrodynamic Institute], Central Aircraft Engine Institute, the Construction Materials Institute, and the Manufacturing Process Institute, but of course the design bureau was in charge of the whole project.

The design work was hard to do, and still continues. This particular aircraft is our child, and the whole design bureau truly loves it immensely! It is important in this country to have a passion for your product, to be interested [in] and enthusiastic about your work. The MiG-21 went through nineteen major modifications, and I am sure the MiG-29 will have a similar long life and will be frequently improved, because we believe the foundation is very good.

But there were two drawbacks to the design: On the first prototype, the nose gear strut was too far forward, and we expected a greater thrust-to-weight ratio. The nose gear strut was moved back from the second prototype on. The weight estimation was a major mistake, but as one American analyst said when we first demonstrated the aircraft in England, the MiG-29 could be about

Mikhail Waldenberg, chief designer for the MiG-29.

2,000lb lighter. If the airframe were that much lighter, there's no telling what it could do! The airframe is so strong that it is impossible for a pilot to break the airframe—not at 9g with missiles on the pylons, not at 12g! At 15g, well, perhaps there would be some deformation of the airframe, but it still would not break. So, I have a long-standing argument with our Air Force about the g-load indicator in the cockpit; if the airframe is limited to, say, 5g, then it makes sense. But if the airframe can tolerate practically any g-load, then there is no need for it; the limitation is in the pilot!

It has much more "energetically sensible" maneuverability than the F-15; its fire-control system is unique; no Western fighter has the same capability. So, there are no major drawbacks or faults in the design.

When the MiG-29 first demonstrated its capabilities at Western air shows in 1988 and 1989, there was a general feeling of awe from the public and some criticism from a few Western manufacturers, particularly the French firm of Dassault. Fighter design is a kind of art, but a competitive one, where one piece of art is intended to destroy another and where lives, money, and reputations are all at risk. So, the French (who were showing off their Rafale fighter) called the media together and said, in effect, "What's the big deal? Of course we could do the same maneuvers, if we wanted to—but why bother? The MiG-29 demonstrates no important combat capabilities that we don't have, too!" Waldenberg and the other Mikoyan representatives responded by challenging the French to fly the routine, if they could—and since the Rafale was a much newer design, how about something better? The French response was essentially no response, and the MiG was the hit of the show. But the incident with the French provided the Russians considerable opportunity to discuss their approach to the design process and the way Western counterparts have traditionally tried to belittle Soviet achievements.

Waldenberg commented on the incident and the comparison of the MiG-29's capabilities to contemporary fighters:

There are many inaccurate reports in Western magazines about our aircraft, particularly about the maneuverability of the MiG-29. For example, I have seen reports comparing the maneuverability of the MiG-29 to the F-18—and [the conclusions are] completely untrue! In my estimation, the only Western fighter that even approaches the agility of the MiG-29 is the F-16C. All others are much inferior, including the F-15. For example, at air shows, where everybody is doing their best to [demonstrate] the best capabilities of the aircraft, we have timed various aircraft executing 360deg turns. I noticed, for example, that the F-16 usually doesn't perform a full 360deg turn, but falls off about 330deg into the maneuver; the MiG-29 executes the turn faster and completes the full turn. The difference is actually one to two seconds. All other aircraft are far inferior. The chief test pilot for Dassault addressed a news conference after our initial appearances at air shows and said, "So the Russians perform a tailslide maneuver; so what? Anyone can perform this." We called the media together and said, "The MiG-29 first flew in 1977. The prototype of the French Rafale fighter first flew in 1986. We had come to see how *new* types of Western aircraft fly, and we discovered that the new types still flew worse than our older ones!" One member of the German parliament got up and wanted to know why they should continue funding the European Fighter Aircraft when even on paper the EFA is inferior to the MiG-29.

If you took into account the time when it was developed and compare the F-15 of those years to the ideas that were introduced and implemented in the MiG-29, the comparison will be even more spectacular. The first flight was in 1977, and the aircraft had been designed much earlier—in 1972—so just at the beginning of the development process those ideas were incorporated into the design. So, the revolutionary capabilities you see now were actually conceived twenty years ago!

Here in the Soviet Union, we in the industry have a lot of influence on the way the specifications are written; we often incorporate technical features that are additional to those asked for by the Air Force, based on our own belief about what is really needed in a new aircraft.

During my first meetings with Western specialists, I was amazed that there were always questions about [whether] this or that super-new system is present in the aircraft. And I always give the same answer to questions about high-technology systems, and that is, "The best system is the one [that is] absent; it cannot malfunction! That is our approach to design work."

You know that the MiG-29 has hydro-mechanical flight controls, and I am frequently asked why there is no fly-by-wire in the MiG-29. We give the following answer to representatives from the high-technology industries, "You have this advanced fly-by-wire technology in your own fighters, so just try to duplicate the flight maneuvers we can do with our old hydraulic and mechanical technology." It is not only words, but the approach of the Mikoyan Design Bureau.

Although I have never seen Western technical requirements for fighters, I believe ours are more complicated than, say, American specifications. For exam-

All dressed up with someplace to go, a two-seat UB model has already fired up and the pilot is now working his way down the short check-list. The UB lacks radar but gains a little periscope, visible over the canopy.

29

ple, when I met General Welch [then US Air Force Chief of Staff] at Farnborough in 1988, and we explained to him the integrated fire-control system incorporated in our fighter, he told us that American industry was just beginning to think of this kind of integration.

Waldenberg and the other Mikoyan employees have been studying Western designs for years, thanks to a long tradition of minimal secrecy about American and British designs. Since the Soviet tradition until very recently was to shoot anybody who said anything about such

defense systems as the MiG, they are used to a lot of basic questions about the airframe, its systems, and its tactical deployment.

Waldenberg provided his own summary of the MiG-29's special features and characteristics, particularly in comparison to Western counterparts:

Guidance to a target is performed by three separate channels; there is a digital data link for secure communications to ground or airborne intercept controllers; also, there is a radar and infrared search-and-track, as well as a helmet-

A previously unpublished photograph of a nonflying mockup in the factory. It lacks the IRST and chaff and flare dispensers, and the nose wheel is two feet farther forward than on the production models. The nose wheel also has a mud guard like that on the Sukhoi-24; production models have a much smaller one. AviaData

mounted sight. The MiG-29 can attack ground targets under visual conditions.

I must add that the powerplants have very good stability, which permits rapid firing of air-to-ground rockets. For example, the aircraft can carry eighty 80mm rockets for use against ground targets; all of those rockets could be launched in one salvo lasting less than one second! The result, of course, is a very unstable airflow into the engines, contaminated with exhaust gasses and particles, yet the powerplant can cope with even this extreme condition without difficulties.

There is an inertial navigation system, but no global positioning system as used on newer Western aircraft. The radio navigation system is designed to be updated by radio beacons and includes provisions for the designation of way-points. Several airfields can be pre-programmed for automatic approach.

The helmet-mounted sight can be used in an integrated mode when selected by the pilot. The helmet-mounted sight then "steers" all the other components of the detection and tracking systems—the IRST, the missile seeker heads, the radar—to the direction of the pilot's sight. It prepares all the components of the fire-control system for instant acquisition and engagement of a target.

The radar is rated to acquire a standard target at a range of 80km [forty-eight miles], but we have been frequently reprimanded about this figure by users of the system! The Indian Air Force demanded, "Why have you announced this figure of 80km, because we continuously acquire targets at 100 or 110km." And we hear the same thing from the Yugoslavian Air Force and the Syrians, too, but it is one of the principles of the company to be very responsible for the figures we provide about the performance of our products. We give our customers guaranteed figures.

We use three types of air-to-air missiles on the aircraft. One is a radar seeker, with 50km range; the second is an infrared seeker, with 20km range; and [the third is] another infrared seeker, with 8–10km range. All the missiles can be fired at a target from all aspects: head-on, tail-on, and crossing engagements. As for the IRST, it has a fifteen-kilometer range for tail-on, nonafterburning targets. We measure range to the target with a laser rangefinder incorporated within the IRST; the laser rangefinder has very good accuracy, as does the angle tracking system of the IRST. These, together, ensure very accurate sighting, so you can use only five rounds from the 30mm cannon to shoot down an aerial target.

Anatoly Kvotchur, one of the leading test pilots in Russia and certainly the most famous after his ejection at the 1989 Paris Air Show. Formerly at Mikoyan, Kvotchur now works at a major research institute in Moscow, improving the cockpits of Russian combat aircraft.

While the MiG demonstrates how well it can plant itself in French soil, Anatoly Kvotchur provides a demonstration of the K-36D ejection seat. Many Western observers contend that no other seat would have functioned successfully under the same conditions. Jon Lake/World Air Power Journal

The gun has 150 rounds in the magazine, and we think that this is much more than necessary, given the accuracy of the whole system. When you consider that each 30mm round weighs about 1kg [over two pounds], this is a serious weight penalty.

All these sighting systems can work together in an integrated way. The radar, in look-down mode, has the same basic capabilities as when looking up. The head-on detection range is, as mentioned, better than 80km; when the target is going away, it is about 50km.

And now, the Luftwaffe has twenty-four MiG-29s in its inventory. They conducted a program of evaluating the aircraft against Western fighters, including the F-15, F-16, and F-18. They might share their results with you, but they certainly won't with *me*. Anyway, the reliability level of the MiG-29 is more than two times higher than the F-15 or F-18; on the other hand, because of current conditions in this country, availability of spares is ten times worse, so this prevents us from absolute [superiority] over our competitors. But we hope this will improve!

Anatoly Kvotchur is one of the greatest test pilots in Russia, one of a small group of men who brought the MiG-29

One of the first test prototypes with the fin extension, deleted in production aircraft. Although the airframe superficially resembles other contemporary designs, the similarity has more to do with mission constraints than piracy. The inclusion of a sophisticated radar, for example, imposes size and shape requirements on the nose of the aircraft; dogfighting and slow-speed agility require massive control surfaces and widely spaced vertical stabilizers.

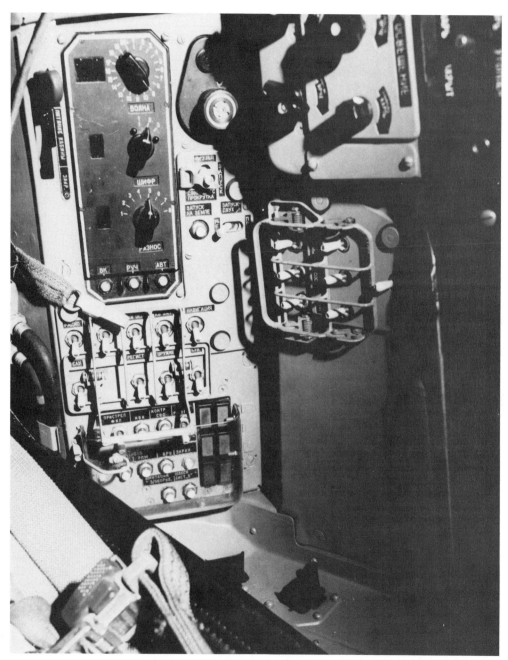

Just a few of the starboard side switches: the control panel for E-502-20 digital data link, cabin air pressure dump control, and circuit breaker management panel (most of the actual breakers are behind the ejection seat, inaccessible during flight).

from its rough-around-the-edges prototype to the fully operational stage. The MiG-29, like any other major aircraft, civilian or military, has undergone a process of development and refinement. The process continues, and Kvotchur is often the pilot who takes an experimental model into the air. A test pilot takes a system from the lab into the real world, puts it through a series of precise evaluations, and then brings it back with data and, sometimes, with advice.

Kvotchur (along with several other test pilots) has also had the honor of introducing the MiG-29 to the West. He demonstrated a bit more of the MiG-29's capabilities than he would have liked when, at the Paris Air Show in 1989, he ejected from his crippled aircraft just before it hit the ground. The crash turned out to be the result of a bird strike, and had the aircraft not been at low level and in full afterburner, the loss of the engine would not have been a problem. It was Kvotchur's first, but not last, ejection from the MiG, and in a perverse sort of way, the performance of the ejection seat under almost-impossible conditions only added to the favorable impression the Western public was developing for the aircraft. (A

After each flight, this recorder is attached via cable to the aircraft, and the flight data for the mission is downloaded for later analysis.

few months later, he and his co-pilot were forced to eject from a two-seat MiG-29, again at low altitude.)

Anatoly Kvotchur:

I am very fond of flying the aircraft, but it is a combat aircraft, designed to fly combat missions. As a test pilot, I need to have a critical approach to every aircraft, because it is my job to discover shortcomings and to suggest improvements. In this sense, an engineering background is important for a test pilot, but at times it tends to take the fun out of flying. Usually, a test pilot for a company should have his own personal opinions about what should and should not be included in the design.

When we began this flight demonstration program in 1989, it was an entirely new activity for our company, so we tried to learn what we could. I made a plan for my own aerobatic routine. We practiced individual maneuvers, [and] then combined them into a complete maneuver. It was quite demanding.

Kvotchur has been one of the demonstration pilots flying the "Cobra" maneuver—where the aircraft rapidly decelerates and hangs motionless in the air for a few moments, before pitching forward again. It is included in the routine to show low-speed handling, but has been sneered at by a few observers, notably the French firm of Dassault.

Kvotchur on the Cobra:

I don't agree with the criticism of the Cobra maneuver as being just a simple trick. It has a function in combat; in the United States, the Rockwell Corporation, in conjunction with a German firm, is working with a super-maneuverable fighter aircraft—the X-31—and [is] exploring exactly the same flight regime. We did research into the handling of the aircraft in rapid deceleration and the ability to point the nose, to acquire targets, and found that the probability of air-to-air launch significantly improves when this maneuver is used. If we consider it as a defensive tactic, we must certainly conclude that an aircraft that can perform it has an advantage over one that can't.

I would say that the MiG-29 has great potential for improvement of engines and airframe. And with a fly-by-wire flight control system and some minor structural modifications, there would be no limitation on angle of attack. I expect to demonstrate such an aircraft in the future.

Kvotchur on cockpit design:

I share the opinion that the MiG-29 cockpit imposes a higher workload on the pilot than Western aircraft, [such as] the F-15E. But at least there is one advantage, and that is that there are not so many points of attention for the pilot; in this sense at least, the MiG-29 is perhaps the most simple in any type of aircraft with similar avionics. Those shortcomings were part of the reason I left Mikoyan and went to work at the Flight Test Institute, where I am now a test pilot but also chief of [the] Ergonomics Laboratory, responsible for man-to-machine interface, [and] where I expect to be able to make positive changes in future designs. From what I've seen of Western fighters, I like the F-16 the best. Although I didn't fly the aircraft, I could tell from sitting in [the] cockpit that the designers did an excellent job.

Sometimes, when specifications are being formulated for a new type of fighter, Ministry of Defense officials and operational pilots are a bit conservative and do not realize what may be possible with new technologies. The success of the new design usually depends greatly on the vision of the designers involved and the test pilots who fly the prototype aircraft. So, the work of a company test

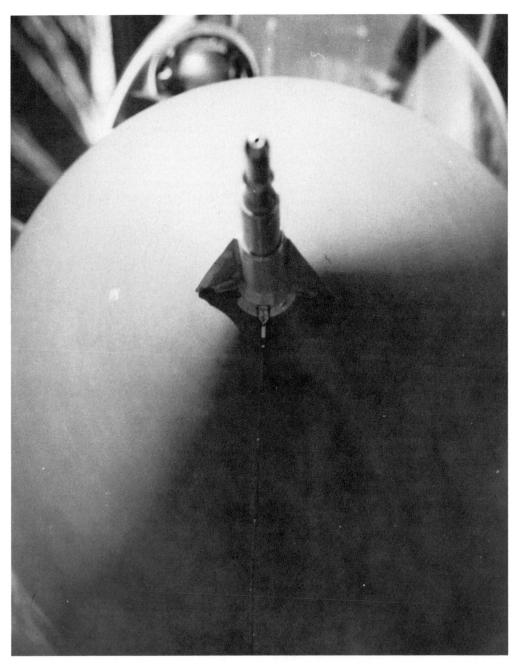

Dominating the Fulcrum's pointy end is this long pitot tube. Note the vortex generators at the pitot's base. These vortex generators en- *hance the MiG-29's stability in high-alpha flight.*

pilot involves participation in the initial design, but [he must also] convince the customer, the military pilots, that their requirements should be formulated with that same kind of vision. On the other side, a test pilot needs to be a representative of the average operational pilot, to be their [liaison] to the designers. It is my job to remind the designers of the needs of the normal pilots, the ones in the operational squadrons.

I think the MiG-29 will be the last fighter aircraft built without fly-by-wire. Everything that can be done with [hydro-mechanical] technology has been included in this aircraft, but to make full use of the fighter's aerodynamic performance, a pilot has to be specially trained. Even a trained pilot has a high workload to make full use of the aircraft's performance. So, I think a MiG-29 can defeat a fly-by-wire fighter, but he would have to work very hard to do it!

Currently, problems of situational awareness are of special concern. Also, [in reducing] pilot workload during engagements [and] ensuring accurate weapon launch, the F-16C and later versions have an advantage over the MiG-29. But there are many factors that make one fighter able to defeat another.

Alexander Velovich is one of several Mikoyan staffers who went to Farnborough for the first Western air show demonstration. Velovich trained as an avionics designer, spent many years working on components of the MiG-29, and is fluent in English, which made him a good candidate to provide interpretation services for the Russian contingent. Although the aircraft has been fairly well described in previous reports, the critical radio, radar, fire-control, and countermeasures systems have been somewhat neglected. So, I asked him to provide some detailed information about these systems.

The heart of the avionics set is the weapons control system (WCS), comprised of two subsystems: RLPK radar sighting system and the OEPRNK-29 electro-optical sighting system. Each of the sighting systems has its own Tz-100 digital computer; [if] one of the systems or its computer [fails,] the other is capable of providing all necessary information for an air-to-air attack mission. The Tz-100 computer has a modest output of just 250,000 effective operations per second, but [that] is reasonably high for a late 1970s piece of equipment.

The MiG-29's WCS does not have a digital databus and software data exchange procedure, called the MIL-STD 1553B—an absolute must for any modern Western fighter. The absence of this technology in our aircraft complicates the job of hardware and software modifications.

The communist system, with its clumsy, bureaucratic way of organizing the defense industry, is to be partly blamed for this. The WCS was divided into two separate subsystems, not to improve performance or reliability, but to put parts of the program under the control of two government agencies, the Ministry of Radio Industry (the RLPK-29) and the Ministry of Aircraft Industry (the OEPRNK-29 sighting system). That made it easier for the Central Committee of the Communist Party to monitor who was responsible for achievements and setbacks and who would get rewards or reprimands from the Party.

Strangely enough, up to now, not a single Western publication has given the correct radar designation for the Fulcrum, widely known as the NO-93, as the result of a short-sighted analyst who misread the stenciling on the aircraft at Farnborough in 1988. Another author caught the error but, in trying to correct it as the NO-193, added a couple [errors] of his own. Actually, the correct designation is the H-019E in Russian. The "H" is the Cyrillic equivalent of an English "N," but the last character is not a number, but the Cyrillic letter [that] begins the Russian word for "export." Moreover, the second character is not an "O" but a

zero, so the proper designation in English is N-019E.

The MiG-29 has a single R-862 radio, which operates in both VHF and UHF. There are 20 channels with frequencies preselected on the ground; the control is a knob on the left console.

Our pilots usually use a call sign similar to those elsewhere: a common word for the squadron, a number for the individual plane—like Falcon 3. A typical radio exchange in an air-to-air engagement would probably include "Tsel vizhoo!," a rough equivalent of "Tally ho!," for visual contact. Then the pilot calls, "Artarkooyu!" which means, "I'm attacking!"

The MiG-29's navigational system is composed of a pair of inertial platforms, redundant to improve reliability, an A323 radio navigation system with instrument landing system (ILS) and TACAN functions. There is also a radio direction finding receiver, a radio beacon receiver, and a radar altimeter. There are two transponders, one for air traffic control functions and one for identification-friend-or-foe (IFF); the IFF system includes an interrogator for use against possible target aircraft.

The radar-warning receiver and chaff and flare dispensers provide reasonable defenses. Unlike most Western aircraft, the MiG uses cartridges that fire upward—a lesson from Afghanistan, where downward-firing flares were useless on low-flying aircraft when heat-seeking missiles were fired from hills.

The MiG-29's only combat experience has been in Operation Desert Storm; it didn't fight in Afghanistan or in the India-Pakistan war as has been previously reported. Although I wouldn't like to comment on the subject, I will repeat the

A MiG-29 flies with two Canadian CF-18As of No. 441 Squadron at the 1989 Abbotsford Air Show. No. 441 Squadron via Jon Lake/World Air Power Journal

story [from] *Flight International* magazine (September 18-24, 1991):

"At the US Navy Tailhook Convention, Sam Sparrowfire relates shooting down a MiG-29. He describes his adversary as being '. . . like a pig looking at a Rolex . . . He loves to look at it, but he doesn't have a clue how it works.' The chairman asks, 'Have we any questions?' A man in the crowd stands up, 'My name is Alexander Vialitch, and I am—how you say?—MiG-29 driver. I would like to thank American pilot for description of MiG-29 and for description of Iraqi pilots!'"

Velovich on working at Mikoyan:

When I graduated from Moscow Aviation Institute, I had only to cross the street to Mikoyan to enter the birthplace of famous Soviet fighters. I did that with deep feeling and great expectations. Now, having worked at Mikoyan for thirteen years and [in] a career from a software programmer to branch manager in [the] Advanced Design Division, in charge of 140 engineers and researchers, I believe I can provide some insights on our work environment. I'll make my comparisons based on observations made at the Fort Worth plant of General Dynamics when we visited there a few years ago.

The MiG-29's RD-33 engine. The powerplant has drawn rave reviews from knowledgeable Western observers like Major Bob Wade, the Canadian Hornet driver who was first to fly the aircraft from the front seat. Major Wade said of the engine, "It's obviously good and reliable, as well as very powerful in afterburner. I was very impressed by engine performance throughout. The engine accelerates just as fast as you want to push the throttle. Even in the tailslide the burners lit off instantaneously and simultaneously. Even by Western standards, it's a tremendous engine." via Jon Lake/World Air Power Journal

First, Mikoyan has just a small fraction of the computer equipment considered necessary by Western firms for the development of a fighter aircraft. Soviet industry, even in the relatively successful aerospace branch, is many years behind the West in CAD/CAM, computer-aided design and manufacture. What is even worse, this gap is widening. Still, Soviet/Russian designers are at least equal in their skill and wit to their Western counterparts. As a rule, they have to be even more resourceful and skillful, because they need to produce a fighter that would match its Western competitor—with much more modest means and equipment at their disposal. Sometimes, this situation leads to intuitive design decisions made with a pencil and paper on your knees, whereas a Western company would spend hours of expensive computer simulation and hundreds of thousands of dollars to achieve results that would be practically the same.

I think the atmosphere in a Western company is much more democratic when you consider relations between staff. At Mikoyan, there are strict rules and a fundamental hierarchy of posts, though in recent years that stiffness has begun to erode. But not too many people

This little bit of mysterious sculpture is positioned just forward of the compressor face. Its function has been reported to be a sensor for inlet airflow, but Jon Lake doubts that it has that function. "It's too far aft to be an air flow indicator," he says, "and people have postulated that it may be an oxygen injector for high altitude relights." The Russians aren't saying.

are capable of making their own decisions without consultation from a higher level.

Of course, there are always [exceptions] and one is Mikhail Waldenberg, chief designer. It was a real pleasure for me to work with this gentleman. I always appreciated his open and creative style of dealing with people and admired his sense of humor. One could easily produce a book of his sayings and jokes and stories, told sometimes during very serious meetings and discussions. Though he became chief designer about halfway through the MiG-29 development process, I think his role in "teaching the bird to fly" was tremendous and decisive. He came to the job at a time when the fighter's development seemed jammed

in numerous misfortunes and delays. His energetic leadership helped to accomplish the flight test program successfully and to introduce the fighter to operational units.

Since I participated in the development of the MiG-29, it has always been interesting to read in Western publications that the Fulcrum's radar was based on stolen APG-65 technology. I wish that were true! Why is it that nobody believes the Westinghouse APQ-164 phased-array radar on the Rockwell B-1B bomber was copied from the MiG-31's radar—the first of that type, introduced years earlier than the APQ-164?

I could offer unusual proof that the MiG-29's designers did their job independently from their Western counterparts.

The MiG-29's N-019E radar, exposed for an industry trade show. This radar is often misidentified in other publications as "NO-93" or "NO-193." via Jon Lake/*World Air Power Journal*

For example, the APG-65 of the F/A-18 Hornet has a wide variety of useful air-to-ground modes; the F-16's APG-66/68 radars are as potent in air-to-ground as they are in air-to-air. Since the dual-role capability is so important, it would have been stupid to omit it if the technology [were] available. And we still don't have an air-to-ground mode on the N-019 radar. As Mikhail Waldenberg likes to say on this subject, "Seeing your neighbor working at his field does not prevent you from pouring sweat while working your own!"

As for the comments that a MiG-29 looks like an F-15 in planform [and] like an F-14 in a front view, is almost the same size as an F/A-18, and [has almost the same] missions as an F-16, I would recommend comparison of a MiG-25 and an F-15. The MiG flew several years earlier than the Western aircraft that resembles it closely. And who is copying whom when you compare the new French Rafale, British-German-Spanish-Italian EFA [European Fighter Aircraft], and Swedish Grippen? It's a fact that similar mission requirements produce similar designs! And it has been true throughout aviation history: Look at the Me 262 and the Gloster Meteor, or the North American F-86 and the MiG-15!"

As with any similar project, years of effort are required before anything tangible happens. Hundreds of people like Waldenberg, Velovich, and Kvotchur plot

A close-up of the antenna of the MiG-29's N-019E radar. via Jon Lake/*World Airpower Journal*

and scheme and argue—just as they do at Grumman, McDonnell Douglas, Boeing, or anywhere else fighters are made. The first MiG-29 flight was made in October 1977, with Mikoyan's then-chief test pilot Alexander Fedotov at the controls. Thirteen prototype aircraft were dedicated to the test program, and Fedotov was soon joined in flying them by Valery Menitsky and others. Testing was conducted at an air base near the town of Ramenskoye. It was here that Western intelligence analysts first set eyes on the new fighter when a spy satellite photographed it on the ramp; excitement about the new air-

frame was almost as intense within the Western intelligence community as it was in Russia, but for different reasons.

The first prototype was the only one with the nose gear well forward, and was used for general evaluation. The second prototype was dedicated to engine tests; one of the lessons the designers learned from that airframe was that the engine mounts weren't strong enough, when one broke on June 16, 1977. The aircraft caught fire and Menitsky had a chance to test the K-36D ejection seat; it worked fine, but the rest of the engine tests would have to be done by another airframe.

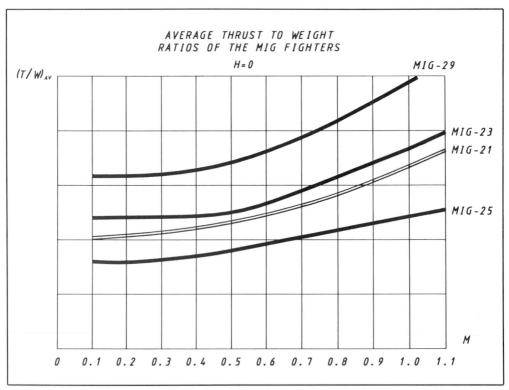

This graph compares the sea-level thrust-to-weight ratios of the MiG-21, MiG-23, MiG-25, and MiG-29 fighters. The MiG-29's thrust-to-weight is greater than one, meaning that its engine produces more pounds of thrust than the aircraft weighs, allowing the Fulcrum to accelerate straight up like a rocket.

Other prototypes were dedicated to testing radar, fire-control, flight characteristics, structural load handling, and other engineering concerns. The fourth of these also caught fire and was abandoned in flight, this time by Fedotov. The flight test program involved the efforts of an informal squadron of test pilots, first from the Mikoyan OKB and then from the Air Force, all wringing out the new systems in search of flaws.

One of the most successful parts of a test program for any fighter is how it will handle at the extremes of its performance envelope. An aircraft can stall at any speed, and a stall (when the wing stops generating lift) generally involves loss of control. Loss of control at low airspeeds often leads to spins, which have killed perhaps more pilots than missiles or guns have. So, the spin part of the test program of any fighter gets special attention, and that's just what happened with the MiG-29.

Spin testing is particularly important in fighters because, unlike other types

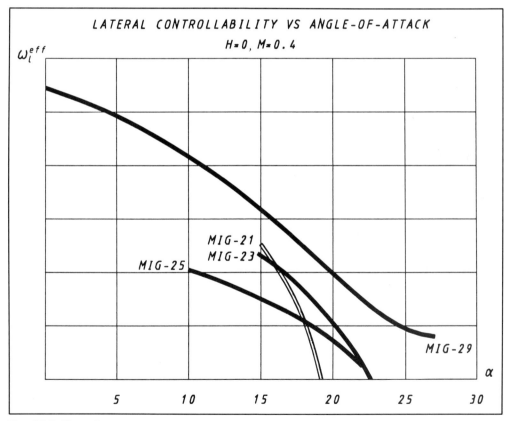

The MiG-29 is known for its agility and controllability at extreme angles of attack. This graph shows how much more roll control the Fulcrum has than the earlier MiGs and how it retains useful control at angles of attack far exceeding those at which the other MiGs depart controlled flight.

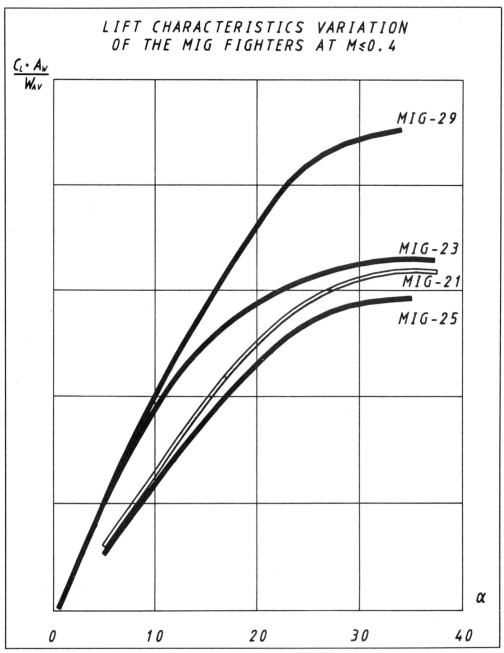

LIFT CHARACTERISTICS VARIATION
OF THE MIG FIGHTERS AT M≤0.4

$$\frac{C_L \cdot A_W}{W_{AV}}$$

MIG-29

MIG-23

MIG-21

MIG-25

α

0   10   20   30   40

*This graph shows how the MiG-29 retains
more lift at extreme angles of attack than the
earlier MiGs.*

that drone steadily through the sky except when landing or taking off, a fighter's work involves a great deal of squirming. Fighters in close engagements or in ground attacks will often fly straight up or down, at full throttle or at idle, at Vne (never exceed airspeed) or at minimum controllable airspeed and very bizarre angles of attack. The process of pointing a gun or a missile seeker head at an enemy takes priority over everything else, and it is not unusual for a fighter engagement to flirt with the risks of stalls and spins.

What the test pilots discovered with the MiG-29 early on was that it stalled like a pig. If you pulled back on the power and increased the alpha, the airplane became more difficult to control. Tiny vortex generators—little wedges of metal—were added to the nose of the airframe, right at the base of the pitot tube, and these deflected just enough airflow to the control surfaces at stall speeds to provide control authority. The vortex generators,

along with other modifications, made the plane virtually spin-proof. It can be forced into a flat spin, but you have to work at it, and, as with a Cessna 152, once you quit trying, it will fly itself out of the spin.

The whole flight control system was designed to make the aircraft easy and safe to fly in combat, or at least as safe as combat flight can be. So, the flight controls incorporate a stall-prevention system that can be overridden, a computer-driven stability augmentation program, and another computer program that adjusts the deflection of the controls based on airspeed and alpha. The result is probably the most controllable fighter in the air.

The first deliveries to the Air Force were made in 1983. Finished aircraft began rolling out of several factories, including the Labor Banner facility in downtown Moscow, in large numbers. Soon, air regiments opposing NATO forces were discarding their old MiG-21s for a new generation of fighter.

Chapter 3

How to Fly the MiG-29

Although the Soviets have been sending MiG-29s to many Western countries for demonstrations and air shows, the aircraft are specially prepared versions, usually without weapons systems and often with cockpits that have been "sterilized" of the latest tactical components. That's not unreasonable. But if you get a chance to visit an air base in Russia, like the one at Kubinka, you can see how the tactical aircraft are maintained and operated.

Kubinka is near Moscow, but far enough away to be deep in the rural Russian countryside. Compared to Amer-

Major General Sokolov, the commander of the air division based at Kubinka.

The wings worn on Sokolov's right breast signify that he has reached the highest level of Soviet fighter-pilot proficiency—Sniper Class.

ican air bases, it is quiet and peaceful, with minimal security, and park-like. Trees line the roads, there is little traffic, and most people get where they're going by walking or riding bikes. It is an old base, started back in the 1930s. Many of the buildings are old, and some are a bit shabby, in need of paint. Maj. Gen. Vladimir Sokolov, the commander of the air division based at Kubinka, apologizes for the condition of the base and explains that there isn't money for the new facilities and the repairs he would like to make. The air division he commands includes several air regiments, or wings, one at Kubinka and the others at three other air bases in the region.

Kubinka hosts the MiG aerobatic team, the Swifts. In the US Air Force, the Thunderbird demonstration team is heavily funded and the pilots are carefully selected and trained for the demanding mission of air show exhibitions. Not so at Kubinka. Members of the Soviet MiG team are operational pilots who perform essentially in their spare time, as volunteers. They've recently received aircraft dedicated to the demonstration mission, with bright paint schemes, but these pilots are, first and foremost, fighter pilots with a combat mission.

The flight line is one long parking area, about a mile from one end to the other. A mixed bag of Aeroflot transports share parking space with Su-24s, Su-25s, Su-27s, and the MiG-29s. The transports are actually in disguise and are used only for military purposes.

A crew chief inspects the latches that secure an air-to-air missile to the MiG. Aircraft are normally parked in dispersal areas and frequently in revetments, as is this one. AviaData

When they are scheduled to fly, the MiGs are towed to the flight line from revetments. Here, the canopy covers are removed and preflight servicing and inspections are done, usually by the crew chief who (unlike his Western counterpart) is a commissioned officer, a lieutenant or captain. Just like his Western counterpart, though, he's a well-trained, skilled, energetic, and professional part of the team. Hours before a flight, the crew chief and his team of enlisted assistants carefully go over the MiGs, inspecting each surface and system. Here's what they see:

Walkaround Inspection

The fighter has a sleek, exotic look to it, even parked on the ramp with the canopy open. It resembles its American contemporary and counterpart, the F-15, in general layout. The wings are straight, with a span of only 37ft; the F-15's span is 43ft. The MiG is 57ft from the pitot tube intake to the trailing edge of the stabilator, and 16ft from the concrete to the top of the vertical stabilizer; the F-15 is 63ft, 9in long and 18ft, 6in tall. The tactical aircraft have a rather pleasing camouflage pattern of dark and light green over gray, punctuated with a bright red star, but the paint usually looks like it was put on with spray cans.

It rather resembles the F-14, F-18, and F-15 fighters, which is somewhat natural. The Soviets were designing a system to compete successfully with those airplanes in combat, so the general re-

The crew chief is an officer in the Russian Air Force, rather than a noncommissioned officer, as in the American military. But the effect is the same: each aircraft is cared for by a career professional dedicated to maintaining the aircraft in a high state of readiness. AviaData

quirements—speed, agility, low speed performance, weapons, and fire-control systems—were the same for everybody. To get the good, all-around visibility needed to see and fight air-to-air, there is no substitute for a high-mounted canopy well forward of the wing. An airborne radar capable of detecting and illuminating targets out to 100km must have a large-enough antenna (about 30in across), which determines the physical size and shape of the front end of the fighter. Air-to-air engagements have always imposed a need for agility at high speeds, during closure and pursuit, and at low-speed "fur balls;" two widely separated vertical stabilizers help the pilot retain control authority when the airspeed bleeds off to almost nothing and the nose has to come left to get a shot off. Two widely spaced engines provide thrust sufficient for Mach 2+ attack or escape, agility in vertical maneuvers, and some protection against battle damage.

RD-33 Engines

The engines are slung low under the wing, well apart, with intake covers for taxi and takeoff, but the covers can be opened for inspection. A peek inside reveals a long, glass-smooth tunnel fabricated from composite material leading to the first-stage fan of the RD-33 turbofan engine. The engine inlets pivot in flight under computer control in response to airspeed and angle-of-attack (alpha).

The "turkey feathers" nozzle assembly that expands and contracts under engine computer control during taxi and flight, augmenting thrust as required by maneuvers.

Although not visible on a walkaround, the engine has a four-stage low-pressure compressor section and a nine-stage high-pressure compressor section, straight-flow combustion chambers, an after-burner, and a variable nozzle similar to those on Western fighters.

The RD-33 engine is really an interesting system, typical of some of the amazing things Soviet designers can do. As the air show "tailslide" demonstrations prove, the RD-33 will reliably keep running when other turbines would stall or shut down. The tailslide is about as extreme a condition as any gas turbine engine will ever encounter, where inlet air pressures—normally very high—drop to virtually zero. When the pilot advances the throttle in such a maneuver, the RD-33 routinely responds promptly and smoothly.

When the MiG first demonstrated the tailslide, it created virtual awe among Western military and industry specialists. One American pilot was asked if he could duplicate such a maneuver in his fighter. He said that he could, but that he would want $35,000 for the performance and would start the maneuver at 30,000ft.

The Russians like the tailslide because it is an easy way to demonstrate that the engine can "take a licking and keep on ticking." In combat, the tailslide is likely to be a very rare maneuver, but the

The wing root extends far forward, up to the cockpit. On its upper surfaces are exhaust vents for the 30mm gun (forward) and the alternate engine air intakes (aft). The alternate intakes are open during some flight maneuvers, as well as during ground operations.

stability of the engine will become extremely important when a very common combat maneuver, missile launches, occurs. Whenever a missile leaves the inboard stations, a plume of rocket gas exhaust is sucked into the engine; at critical phases of combat maneuvers, this exhaust can affect engine performance. The Soviet engine designers seem to have succeeded in assembling a powerplant that is extremely responsive and reliable. But it does have a couple of disadvantages. One is that it generates a visible smoke plume when power settings are changed, making the fighter more visible in combat. Another is that the rated life of the engine is only 1,000hr, while typical Western models last much longer. One

reason offered for the short time between overhauls is that the Soviets traditionally use artificially short cycles for critical components to make sure there is always considerable life left in every part of an operational aircraft. Another possible reason is that the engines just wear out quickly.

The RD-33 appears to run hotter than equivalent Western turbojets, which seems to be how the pilots coax all that power out of it. Western pilots who've flown the MiG-29 say that the engine seems a bit less powerful than NATO equivalents in what is usually called "dry" or "military power," which means full throttle without benefit of afterburners. They also say that it is more powerful

The afterburner pumps large quantities of fuel through this assembly. The result is tremendous power and a tremendous loss of fuel economy.

when advanced to afterburner and that the transition is smoother and more rapid than in F-15s or F-18s.

Fuselage and Wings

Viewed from the side, the whole aircraft seems to be an airfoil—and it is. The fuselage contributes a large portion (about forty percent) of the lift required for flight. When viewed from above, it becomes apparent that the fuselage flows smoothly outward to the wingtip without any clear separation of one from the other. It is constructed of composites, titanium alloys, and aluminum.

The wing roots blend into the fuselage in a way that resembles the F-18,

extending forward to the cockpit. On their upper surfaces are the secondary air inlets that provide airflow to the engines during taxi and takeoff. These inlets also open during some flight maneuvers, and there has been speculation that they're partially responsible for the engine's ability to respond smoothly under conditions that make others stall or stumble.

An exploration of the aircraft's exterior will reveal a large collection of sensors, antennas, aerials, fittings, and housings, all of which indicate what's going on. Perhaps the most important of these is a glass sphere just to the front of the windscreen and to starboard of center. This is the magical eye of the infrared

The first stage of the R-33 is visible down the long, smooth tunnel of the engine intake—if the door is open. Much of the MiG-29's smooth *performance under adverse conditions has been attributed to excellent intake design.*

seek-and-track (IRST) sensor; collimated with the sensor is a powerful laser. The whole package is designated "Object 138" or KOLS by Mikoyan. Inside the sphere is a mirror that rotates, scanning the skies for thermal signatures. Air data sensors attached to the fuselage include an alpha sensor just aft of the radome, a dynamic pressure probe, and the pitot tube extending well forward of the radome.

The point where the pitot tube joins the nose of the aircraft is reinforced by two small metal gussets. A casual observer would think they are simply there to strengthen the long tube, but their importance is actually much greater. At low speeds and high alpha, these little components disrupt the airflow, creating vortexes that feed enough air to the rudders and stabilizers to give the aircraft control authority when it would otherwise thrash around the sky.

Also forward of the windscreen, but to port of center is an identification-friend-or-foe (IFF) antenna; a similar unit it attached at the same point underneath the aircraft. In the same general vicinity, around the radar bay, are antennas for the instrument landing system (ILS) receiver and UHF transmitter. Further aft, in the left wing root extension alongside the cannon, is an electronic countermeasures antenna. Just aft of the canopy, over the electronic equipment bays, are several other antennas for radios and the ADF (automatic direction finder) system.

The airframe is designed as one seamless airfoil, the fuselage area contributing a huge forty percent of the lift produced. The alternate engine air intakes are clearly visible. AviaData

Major Bob Wade Interview

Canadian Major Wade was the first Western military pilot to fly the MiG-29; these remarks were recorded shortly after that flight.

Mikoyan is marketing the MiG-29 to break into Western markets, and to do that they need to develop credibility in their fighter—to show the public that it is comparable in performance to Western fighters. They've been more than successful in doing that.

It uses a different design approach than Western designs, in the sense that the Mikoyan Design Bureau kept everything as simple as possible. It won't necessarily last twenty years, but it is very, very capable. They are achieving the same kind of flight performance that fly-by-wire systems do, primarily because of better thrust-to-weight ratios than that of Western aircraft and better design.

It took a lot more effort to achieve the same flight maneuvers in the MiG-29 than would be required in an F-18, for example. To accomplish the same job you just have to fly the airplane the whole time; you always need a lot of rudder coordination at slow speeds, you need a lot of aileron to pick up the wing as it drops. The control is there—it is available to you—but in the F-18 the fly-by-wire looks after it. In the MiG-29 the pilot has to make the input.

The control forces are different. In the F-18 you have an artificial feel which is very smooth and quite light, whereas you have a twenty-eight pound stick

Canadian Major Bob Wade with Mikoyan test pilot Valery Menitsky in the officers' club at

Royal Canadian Air Force Station Comox after Wade's July 1990 flight in the MiG-29.

force in the MiG and the control column is slightly higher and a bit farther forward. It wasn't difficult and you don't have to be super strong to do it; it just feels different.

I enjoyed it tremendously. I was amazed at how agile that fighter was, the ability to point the nose. It would be a tremendous turn fighter. I'm not allowed to go public and make any direct comparisons with any Western fighters, but what I can say is that its' performance at the low-speed end of the flight envelope is equal to or superior to anything demonstrated by Western display pilots.

The engine accelerates as fast as you want to push the throttle. By Western standards it's an outstanding engine—a great engine! I was very impressed by the engine performance throughout. I don't believe it produces as much power in the military power setting, but it has a tremendous increase in afterburner. It's obviously good, it's reliable, the exhaust gas temperatures and rpms were very similar to those of the General Electric 404 engine.

I did a low-speed loop from about 350 km/h and it was no problem for the airplane at all—lots of power to get around. Again, at low speed it required a lot of aileron and rudder input, and I could feel Valery [the Russian pilot] overriding me on the controls, helping me out. But it was very, very benign and easy to fly. Then Valery executed two hammerhead stall turns. There are not many high-performance aircraft that will

do that. He did two of these, below 2,000 feet, to the left, which surprised me because engine torque should make them much easier to do to the right. They've never demonstrated this turn in the air show routine—I would certainly incorporate the maneuver in my routine *if* the F-18 would do it!

I think it takes more pilot expertise to accomplish the same type of performance as a Western fighter—you're busier flying the airplane than you would be in a Western fighter. I think the MiG-29 doesn't display information as well. Are you busy flying the airplane or are you busy operating the weapons systems?

They cut corners where they can. They're very performance oriented. They are less sophisticated with the design than Western fighters but they achieve tremendous results. You look at Western fighters—hardly any incorporate IRST yet it offers tremendous capability; you can do a passive intercept with it, without alerting your target. And the MiG has a data link. How many Western fighters have it? RAW (radar attack warning) gear—some of our airplanes have it, but not all. The laser rangefinder incorporated with the gun makes it a very accurate system. With that airplane's turn performance the gun is a very, very viable weapon because a lot of its kill capablity will be within missile minimum range where you have a tremendous advantage with an accurate gun.

Control surfaces and fin panels are constructed of carbon fiber.

The wings are mostly aluminum, but critical components are made of titanium alloy. The structure is based on three massive spars, the foundation of a torsion box assembly that gives the airframe nearly unbreakable strength.

External Stores

Three pylons on each wing will accept a wide variety of missiles, bombs, fuel tanks, and rocket pods. Although the AA-10 and AA-11 missiles are most common for the basic air-to-air mission, for ground attack, the Fulcrum can be fitted with four 32×57mm or 18×80mm rocket pods with eighteen rockets in each pod. For ferry flights, a centerline fuel tank can be added between the engines, along with additional tanks on the wings.

Tail

The massive vertical stabilizers each wear a bright red star and an assortment of antennas. The tip of the starboard fin incorporates a VHF antenna, a radar-warning receiver antenna, and an antenna for the ILS system with the NATO code-name "Swift Rod." The port fin houses the Sirena-3 electronics countermeasures antenna. Both fins have extensions housing dispensers for chaff and flare cartridges;

in combat, the countermeasures system will fire bundles of radar-reflecting chaff to spoof radar-guided missiles and flares to decoy infrared missiles away from the aircraft.

Using two vertical stabilizers has several advantages: a smaller radar signature, improved control authority in some low-speed maneuvers, and lighter weight for the same fin area.

The aircraft uses massive horizontal stabilators rather than stabilizers and elevators. The huge control area is another reason for the excellent handling qualities at low-airspeed, high-alpha conditions, as found in close combat.

One of the major shortcomings of the MiG-29 is the low position of the pilot. In a fighter, where the ability to see an adversary remains an essential for successful combat, a pilot should have a large and unobstructed field of view. The MiG pilot's view is good to the rear (thanks to the canopy design and three large mirrors on the canopy bow) and front (thanks to a single-piece windscreen and despite the HUD), but is poor for targets coming up from below.

The control column grip incorporates six controls (in front and not visible in this shot is the trigger that launches weapons that have been selected and armed): 1.) HUD target symbology control, used for target designation on the heads-up display; 2.) emergency autopilot disengage switch; 3.) trim control; *4.) "panic" switch—pushing this button initiates an autopilot maneuver that will bring the aircraft to straight and level from any attitude, no matter how extreme, making MiG-29 instructor pilots the envy of their profession; 5.) "squack" button for the IFF/radar transponder.*

Landing Gear

The landing gear are quite conventional. The nose gear incorporates two wheels and a small mud guard and is placed just forward of the engine air intakes. The nose gear is steerable through 8deg for takeoff and through 30deg for taxi if the switch on the control column is engaged.

A tank for de-icing fluid is attached to the nose wheel door. The fluid that goes in the tank is 200-proof alcohol, and the crews that come by to top off the aircraft's tank cheerfully offer to top off the tanks of any observers, as well.

The main gear are conventionally placed in approximate mid-span of the wing, where it joins the fuselage. But the gear design provides very little clearance for the engine exhausts on landing and takeoff, so student pilots (and journeymen ones as well) take particular care to avoid over-rotating the aircraft.

Cockpit

The MiG is mounted pretty much like any fighter, up a ladder. The Russians, who expect to get their feet muddy, installed a boot brush on the ladder to encourage the pilot to keep the office tidy.

K-36D ejection seat handles are located between the pilot's thighs, unlike the Martin-Baker seats used by the American and British fighters, where the handles are by the hips and overhead. If you give the handles a good pull and the seat has been armed, the canopy will blow off the aircraft, and the seat will rocket away and up (regardless of the aircraft's attitude at ejection). Appearing when the handles come up is a blast deflector, part of which is visible here with a warning sign attached.

It is about a 10ft climb up to the cockpit. Once at the top, the pilot checks to ensure the ejection seat is still safetied with its pins and cords in place, and then steps down onto the seat and slides into place.

The K-36D seat is hard and the back is reclined slightly. Up around the pilot's shoulders will be the drogue parachute assemblies; taller pilots will feel them.

Ejection Seat

Anatoly Kvotchur was showing off to the crowd at Paris in the summer of 1989, flying low and slow, demonstrating minimum airspeed controllability. About the time he advanced the throttle to full afterburner, the right engine sucked up enough birds to flame it out. Ordinarily, having one engine quit is not a catastrophe—an entire mission can normally be flown with just one of the two—but the combination of low speed, low altitude, and the engine in full afterburner trying to push the aircraft to the right made for an uncontrollable situation. It didn't take Kvotchur long to decide it was time to leave, and he reached down to the red handles and pulled. The jet drove itself into the French landscape safely away from the crowd, while Kvotchur continued to entertain with his low-altitude, pilot-leaves-the-airplane stunt. He was so low that the canopy didn't inflate fully before he was deposited in front of the crowd.

Such events ordinarily are unmitigated disasters, but this one was different. For one thing, nobody was killed or even

An overview of the MiG-29 cockpit showing the K-36D seat, complete with safety pins. It's a tight fit compared to some other fighters, and a hard seat—not the cockpit of choice for those long ferry flights to distant battlefields. And, if you're tall, the drogue arm assemblies below the headrest will dig into your shoulders.

hurt. The aircraft was a total loss (which probably pleased some of the MiG's competitors), but the second aircraft, a two-seat B model, carried on with the display. The crowd of experts and enthusiasts, alike, were impressed with the ability of the ejection seat to perform under nearly impossible conditions, an aircraft that was nearly vertical and low, and a pilot struggling to gain control. It took a while before the cause of the incident was discovered, but whatever the reason for

the engine failure, at least the K-36D seat performed flawlessly.

The K-36D seat is similar to other "zero-zero" (capable of saving the pilot at zero speed and zero altitude) seats in operation; the system is armed by removing several pins from switches in the cockpit and can be operated even when the aircraft is sitting on the runway or at altitudes of many thousands of feet. Unlike Western seats which offer several handles, the K-36D has only one, just aft of

Left console controls: 1.) the throttle slides fore and aft, with 2.) buttons to select short- or long-range missiles, 3.) radio transmit button, 4.) a dual-purpose button for radar lock control/nose wheel steering control, and 5.) air brake control. To the front are the 6.) landing gear selector, 7.) canopy control and armament control panel, 8.) engine control panel, 9.) controls for radio compass, 10.)
flaps, 11.) VHF radio, 12.) oxygen, 13.) controls for drag parachute release, emergency nose wheel steering, stick force, emergency hydraulic pressure, and 14.) the throttle friction lever. To the right of the canopy lock are 15.) controls for stand-by weapons release, 16.) radar mode selection, and 17.) rudder trim.

the stick. A sharp tug begins a series of events: The canopy is blown off, and the pilot's feet are pulled back against the seat. At the same time and for the same reason, an air deflector comes up between the pilot's legs, and two panels drop down along his upper arms and elbows; all of this protects against the sudden exposure to the slipstream. Injuries in ejections are the rule, rather than the exception, and the K-36D seat is designed to reduce the thrashing around that results from popping into a 500mph blast of air. A pilot normally keeps his visor down, day or night; with the oxygen mask and helmet, this provides some protection, too.

The seat is programmed to allow the canopy to clear the aircraft; then, rocket motors under the seat fire and carry the seat assembly clear. At this point, the seat is a wholly self-contained (and short-lived) aircraft, with a single mission to perform. Incorporated into the seat are sensors that tell which way is up, and the seat "flies" upward, even if the ejection was from an inverted aircraft, as happened to Kvotchur. The rocket motors burn out quickly, and then the parachute deployment cycle begins. The K-36D seat is a bit unusual; it has two arms projecting from the area just above the pilot's shoulders, with small, drogue parachutes at the

In addition to the standard mix of conventional instruments for 1.) attitude reference, 2.) horizontal reference, 3.) fuel quantity and flow, 4.) exhaust gas temperature, and 5.) radar altimeter, there is a 6.) panel for the integrated weapons systems (radar, IRST, *helmet-mounted sight, and laser rangefinder) and a 7.) radar display; 8.) head position sensors below the HUD are part of the helmet-mounted sight system, 9.) airspeed, 10.) barometric altimeter and 11.) combination instrument for turn and slip/vertical velocity.*

The smooth, sleek wing tip sports a static-discharge device.

ends. These stabilize the seat and prevent tumbling. Then, the pilot separates from the seat, and the parachute lines and canopy deploy from their storage areas in the seatback and headrest. The drag from the parachute begins to slow the pilot; at high speeds, the deployment process is programmed by sensors in the seat to be far more gradual than at low speeds and altitudes. Finally, the parachute inflates and the ejection seat falls away.

Anatoly Kvotchur has had occasion to use the K-36D; here's what he has to say about the experience:

I have ejected twice, and both were with the standard K-36D seat, one of the best in the world—certainly, the best in this country! The seat provides not only the possibility of saving the pilot's life, but saving his experience, too. It isn't perfect and I am aware of some short-comings . . . but safety in the system isn't just the seat, but the mechanism for removing the canopy, the sequencing of delays from the moment you pull the handle—plus, of course, the cockpit indicators that tell a pilot that it is about time for him to leave his horse!

In both ejections, I was in very ex-treme conditions, at low altitude. Of course, it is very unpleasant to leave an aircraft. The sensation of ejection was very smooth, and I was aware of every-thing that was happening. My eyes stayed open, and I saw the aircraft separating from me, rather than the other way around! The first time was so

The main circuit breaker panel is aft of the ejection seat and cannot be reached while in flight.

low that there wasn't enough time for the parachute to fully open and I had a strong impact with the ground.

Strapping In

Russian pilots wear their flight suits over their "speed jeans" or g-suits. Like other fighter pilots, they wear a complicated parachute harness that buckles to the seat. Once they are in the cockpit, the crew chief makes sure the buckles are secure and helps connect the fittings for the speed jeans, oxygen mask, and the connectors for the microphone (in the mask) and headset (in the helmet). The mask and helmet are both beautifully made, light and comfortable compared to

American models. The helmet is so comfortable that Russian pilots don't pry theirs off at the first opportunity, as do F-15 and F-18 pilots; on the other hand, the protection of the lighter helmet is probably less, too.

The cockpit is quite similar to any American single-seat fighter of the 1960s or 1970s: a standard instrument panel with lots of very conventional gauges and switches, a heads-up display (HUD) in the usual spot, throttle convenient to the left hand and a stick between your knees, topped with the usual assortment of buttons and triggers. Just in front of the seat are two large, red, flexible handles that operate the ejection seat.

The tip of the starboard fin houses the VHF antenna. The rounded fairing below it houses the radar warning receiver. The spear-shaped device is the ILS antenna, and below it are two static-discharge devices—one on the fin and one on the rudder.

The cockpit is actually the MiG's major handicap. Even Mikoyan and the test pilots, including Kvotchur, will tell you that it is an older-generation solution and that newer fighters such as the F-15E Strike Eagle, with its "glass cockpit" approach, are much better. Under the same conditions, a MiG pilot's workload is higher than an Eagle pilot's, the result of having to look at many instruments in many places. Newer aircraft such as the Strike Eagle now use three or four cathode ray tube (TV screen) displays, programmed to show selected information on demand; the result is a very simple panel. When all critical data can be sent to the HUD, a pilot scarcely needs to look in the cockpit at all.

The panel may not be exactly state-of-the-art, but it shares the technology of many other combat aircraft still in service and it works. The instruments are in the same positions as those of any older Western plane: Artificial horizon and engine instruments cover most of the front panel, and the functions of most are obvious even if the legends are printed in Cyrillic letters.

The left console includes the throttle, which slides fore and aft on rods. Buttons and switches for the air brakes, radio, and radar-target lock are part of the throttle grip. The left cockpit panel also includes the gear lever, radar and armament controls, oxygen system and radio controls, and autopilot console.

The control column includes a trim switch button, IFF interrogation switch, trigger for weapons release, radar missile control, autopilot disengage, and a "panic" switch. The latter will, when pushed and if enough altitude remains, return the aircraft to wings-level horizontal flight regardless of what attitude the airplane is in.

The right console incorporates the keypad for data entry into the computer, the navigation and engine ignition controls, and radio switches.

As the design has evolved, a wide variety of minor adjustments in cockpit layout have been made. Some aircraft will have the engine ignition panel (or the INS or radio switches, or warning panel) set up differently, but the arrangement is always fundamentally the same, both in the MiG and Sukhoi interceptor. There are

The IFF antennas are located on the port side, aft of the radome.

some great advantages to the tradition, one of which is that for most pilots, transition from one airframe design to another is extremely simple. For example, when Anatoly Kvotchur got checked out in the Sukhoi-27 after a long career as Mikoyan's test pilot, he got a familiarization ride in the two-seat trainer, then on his second flight was practicing demonstration maneuvers, and on his sixth flight was performing in an air show. That's tough to do if the pilot doesn't know where the airspeed indicator is.

Directly below the HUD, at the top of the panel, are two sensors for the helmet-mounted sight system. To the left are the controls for armament systems, and to the right are the radar screen and warning panel.

Around the Patch

And now, for a practice flight. The crew chief has made sure everything's set up, so all you have to do is reach over on the right side of the seat; the engine ignition panel switch goes to START (*ZAPUSK* to the Russians), the starboard engine—Number One—is selected. The ignition system uses electrical power, which can come from an internal battery, one of the ground support vehicles equipped with cables on the ramp, or outlets at each of the parking spaces. (Most Western fighters use hydraulic power, either from a special start cart or from a built-in accumulator.)

Now, advance the throttle from STOP to *MALY GAS*, the Russian equivalent of IDLE. Just as in other fighter aircraft, this

Although some Western observers have referred to various details of the MiG's construction as "crude," most seem perfectly normal and conventional for an older design. This plumbing for the port side main gear door is effective, efficient, durable, and the result of an assembly line that cranked out more than 800 versions of the same item.

begins the start sequence and there is nothing more for the pilot to do except keep an eye on the process and make sure nothing goes awry. The engine will spin up to about thirty percent before any fuel is injected by the engine control computer; then, with enough airflow for the turbine to breathe, it lights off. If you were doing this in an F-15, the rpm and engine sound would slowly, gradually build, but with the MiG and the RD-33, the engine lights off with a sudden whoosh, a rapid rise in rpm and a jolt of power that pushes the nose down against the gear.

Unless there is an overspeed or over-temp—both of which are rare with the RD-33—the engine is quickly up to speed

and the electrical umbilical can be removed. The left engine is selected and started with internal power, and in a very short time you are in business. Unless you need the inertial navigation system initialized (a 10min process, East or West), the canopy can be locked with the latch on the left rail. Signal the crew chief to pull the chocks, release the parking brake, and ease off on the toe brakes (incorporated into the rudder pedals). There is plenty of thrust to taxi out of the spot, and by using the steerable nose wheel, you trundle out onto the taxiway to the runway. Russian pilots taxi much faster than American fighter pilots do, and arrive at the departure end of the runway very

There aren't any steps built into the side of the MiG-29, as with Western models, so a ladder is usually used. An alternative, though, is to climb up on the tail, back by the engine exhaust nozzles, and then carefully navigate along the slippery slope of the wing roots to the cockpit—a dangerous maneuver but one the Russian pilots seem to do with confidence.

quickly. An F-16 gets a thorough examination by a horde of ordnance technicians at the "last chance" position before taking to the active; traffic and tower permitting, Russian pilots get a quick once-over, roll onto the runway, and go.

So, we get takeoff clearance, roll out onto the runway, and hold with full application of the brakes. Advance the throttle

Colonel Alexander Kutuzov prepares to lead the MiG demonstration team, the Swifts, aloft for a practice session. The Russian demonstration teams are part-time activities, unlike the Blue Angels or Red Arrows.

full forward; it will stop at what we call military power (*MAXIMAL* to the Russians). In the center of the throttle quadrant is a sliding latch; lift it with your middle finger and continue to apply pressure—and you're in afterburner. You can't see it from the cockpit, but twin tongues of flame extend 20ft behind the jet; the rumble of their power penetrates clearly through the controls.

Brakes off! The jet moves off smoothly, accelerating rapidly. If you've lined up carefully on the centerline, the aircraft shouldn't wander much. Steer with the pedals—just a touch, as required to stay on the center-line. At about sixty knots, the rudders will start to provide control authority; continue to track the centerline, and at about 110 knots, smoothly bring the stick back. Be careful not to overrotate; remember those low-slung engine nozzles! The nose comes up and the MiG-29 follows, accelerating rapidly. You're off the deck in less than 1000ft of runway, at about 125 knots.

If you wanted to stay in afterburner, you could keep the nose coming back until it was pointed straight up and then head for outer space—and accelerate rapidly while doing it. That's usually a poor fuel-management technique, though, so we'll just throttle back out of afterburner; *MAXIMAL* is still good for a comfortable rate of climb without strain, and consumes about half the fuel.

The gear select handle is in the same place as it is in just about every other fighter: on the left side of the panel, where you won't forget about it. Raise the handle, and the wheels come up and stow themselves with a "thunk."

The leading edge slats and the flaps provide extra lift at low speeds. The slats come and go when the flight control computer tells them to; the pilot controls only the flaps, operated by a button on the left console. Cleaned up now, the MiG

*Ground crewmen hook up a tow bar to one of
the Swifts' Fulcrums prior to a practice hop.*

vaults upward. Push the stick forward and level out at 3,000m. With a throttle setting of *MAXIMAL* and a level attitude, the airspeed will quickly build to about Mach 0.75. The sensation is of quiet power.

Roll in a little aileron and the aircraft will roll around its axis at about 270deg per second. Bring the wings level; still in *MAXIMAL* throttle, pull back on the stick to bring up the nose at about 30deg per second and maintain about a 4g pull-up. The maneuver will start at about 500kph and, with constant throttle airspeed, will decay to about 180kph. If you do it right, you'll feel the bump as you go through your own wake at the bottom of the loop, back where you started.

The famous tailslide begins like a loop, but with the throttle back at idle. Raise the nose to about 75deg, and you'll come up about 500ft and hover for a moment before sliding back toward earth.

If you apply throttle all the way into afterburner as you reach the top, the slide will be minimal. Push forward on the control column to pitch forward back to straight and level. Unlike many other fighters, the MiG remains controllable under these extreme conditions, although with no airflow over the control surfaces in the slide, the plane wallows like a pig.

For the return trip, the pattern altitude is 600m. Call the tower for landing clearance and instructions, then enter the ILS on a straight-in approach, at 500kph indicated airspeed. Drop the gear, flaps, and airbrake. The HUD will provide the instrument landing system cues; if you stay lined up, it will deposit you at the end of the runway, with an air speed of about 230kph. Use the throttle as required to maintain the glideslope. You can pop the drag parachute before the wheels touch, but don't raise the nose much to bleed off

A trio of Fulcrums swoop above the runway during practice for an air show. The demonstration team pilots are all members of a regular combat wing, their air show performances are in addition to the normal routine training.

Overhead, in the middle of their air show routine, the MiG team display the aircraft's layout. These all have center line gas tanks installed.

Six Fulcrums in demonstration team colors blast over the field at the bottom of a loop. The routine is low, fast, precise, and very loud.

Demonstration aircraft share the ramp with the combat aircraft, and other than for the *paint schemes there don't seem to be many differences.*

excess airspeed; the clearance for the tailpipes is tiny, and it is very easy to drag them on the concrete. An F-15 can pull the nose way up after touchdown, using the wings and fuselage as a massive air brake, but that won't work with the MiG. Roll out is about 2,000ft.

With the parachute and airbrakes out, you'll touch down at about 125 knots, and the aircraft will slow. A ground crew-

A pair of Fulcrums fly formation with a Tu-95 Bear and an Il-76 Candid tanker. The display is part of an air show routine, not a tactical *display; the MiGs normally keep safely away from such proceedings.*

De-icing fluid consisting of 200-proof alcohol is often used to thaw the ground crew as well as the aircraft.

Short final—leading edge slats out, big landing light on, a Fulcrum comes back to Kubinka's long runway.

Gear down, flaps down, periscope up, and nozzles assymetrical—a UB trainer crosses the numbers.

man will be waiting at the midpoint of the field for the drag parachute, which is jettisoned before you taxi back to the parking spot on the ramp.

Retard the throttles to STOP, and the engine will automatically shut down. One of the ground crew will roll a small cart over and attach a cable to a receptacle on

A Fulcrum C about as flared as you want to get—any more rotation scrapes the nozzles on the runway. The fin extensions are obvious here; their only function is to house the flare and chaff dispensers.

The MiG-29 lands so "hot" and has so little clearance for the exhaust nozzles that a braking parachute is an absolute essential. A spherical device covers the large, strong, efficient cruciform braking parachute that the pilot releases on landing. In fact, the parachute can be deployed in the air at 150 knots, as the demonstration pilots sometimes do at shows.

The drag parachute deploys with a loud "pop" and quickly slows the slippery jet from flight speed to a more sedate pace suitable for taxiing back to the barn. AviaData

One of the newer "hump-backed" Fulcrum Cs taxis in from a bit of fun and games. The hump houses additional fuel and avionics.

After slowing the MiG, the chute is jettisoned. A ground crewman retrieves the chute and repacks it for the next flight.

the underside of the aircraft near the tail and then switch on the device. The cart contains a data recorder that transfers to magnetic tape information about the aircraft's systems' performance during the flight for later analysis by the maintenance office. At Kubinka, this task is performed by three women, civilian employees who are married to Air Force officers at the base.

After a routine flight, the pilot normally hops out of the aircraft, signs off on the flight while discussing any problems with the crew chief, and then immediately begins a de-briefing with his wingman. This de-briefing usually starts right on the ramp and continues in the operations building—sometimes taking longer than the flight itself.

In this view, the starboard intake cover is open and the port cover is closed. These covers are normally closed during landing and any time the aircraft is on the ground to prevent rocks or other foreign objects from being ingested by the engine.

Chapter 4

Weapons

A modern fighter has to be prepared for engagements at long, intermediate, and close ranges, each of which requires different strategies, tactics, and weapons. The emphasis for the last few decades has been away from close encounters and toward beyond-visual-range shots with guided missiles.

The MiG, like its Western contemporaries, was designed to be able to detect, designate, and destroy targets at long range with radar-based technology. The MiG has a powerful N-019 radar, code-named by NATO as "Slot Back," which appears to be inspired by the American APG-63 and APG-65 systems used on the F-15C and F/A-18C, respectively. This type of radar can be adjusted to cope with targets under different tactical conditions and, unlike older radars, uses Doppler and

This is what it's all about: a Fulcrum ready for anything; the big missiles inboard are semi-active radar-homing AA-10s with beyond-visual-range capability. Outboard are AA-8s, the older version of the Russian heat-seeker. They've been replaced by the AA-11, which *looks about the same, but is far more agile and sensitive and is an all-aspect advanced dog-fighting missile. For those really close encounters, there is still the superb 30mm gun (on the other side).* AviaData

Above and Above Right
The AA-11 advanced air-to-air missile (on a Su-27) is a product of decades of research and development of rocket motor and guidance technologies. The rounded nose is translucent, covering a very sensitive seeker head. Just behind it are four angle-of-attack sensors that provide data to the missile's computer. Two sets of control fins and exhaust vector vanes make the AA-11 an extremely squirmy and hazardous weapons system.

The helmet-mounted sight steers the IRST, missile seeker heads, and radar, providing quick weapons lock-on—a decisive advantage in combat.

A pair of Fulcrums take to the Russian skies, a single-seat A model leading a two-seat *trainer; both are in the livery of the MiG-29 demonstration team, the Swifts.*

pulse rate technologies to pick out movement against the ground clutter that used to hide adversaries.

Once a target appears on the radar, it can be displayed on the heads-up display (HUD), interrogated with identification-friend-or-foe (IFF), and engaged at ranges of about 100km/60 miles with radar-homing missiles. The Russian big stick in this department is the AA-10A Alamo (NATO

These 30mm rounds are ready for loading. That's enough ammunition to destroy at least two aerial targets, according to Mikoyan.

codename), which Western intelligence experts rate at 25km but probably will score at much longer ranges.

The problem with radar, though, is that it telegraphs the punch and encourages countermeasures. Modern fighters carry radar-warning receivers that immediately indicate when an adversary is "painting" him and from what direction. This typically results in the targeted victim turning away, punching chaff, and sometimes trying to get down close to the deck where radar lock is easier to break. It also sometimes results in the victim becoming annoyed and initiating an attack of his own.

The AA-10, though, is a big, long-range missile that carries a warhead large enough to destroy an aircraft with a near miss. It comes in two basic versions: one, semi-active radar-homing (the A model)

and the other, a passive infrared (IR) seeker (the B model). The AA-10B has the advantage of long range and Stealth; its seeker head is programmed to steer toward jet exhaust only, and the only thing that can spook it is a flare launched at just the right moment. The A-model Alamo is an all-aspect missile that can be launched at a target head-on, tail-on, or crossing. And, because the radar, IRST system, and the helmet-mounted sight are integrated, the missile can be launched at targets off to the side of the aircraft as well as straight ahead.

Aircraft designers once thought dogfights with guns and short-range missiles were history. Then, in Vietnam, MiG fighters began engaging and frequently defeating American F-4 Phantom fighters in dogfights when long-range missiles wouldn't work. The experience quickly

The full menu of weapons for the Fulcrum laid out in a German aircraft shelter; 80mm rockets, a full load of 149 30mm rounds for the gun, Archers and Aphids for almost any social engagement. via Jon Lake/*World Air Power Journal*

resulted in a strap-on gun for the Phantom (which had been designed without one) and validated Mikoyan's commitment to guns and IR missiles.

So, the MiG carries an IR-seeking missile with its "fire and forget" talent for knocking adversaries out of the air at ranges too close for the radar-guided models. This was (and sometimes still is) the AA-8 Aphid, with a range of only about 3km. The Aphid is fast and maneuverable, but needs to be launched at the rear of a target, where the engine heat signature is strongest, for reliable hits.

The AA-8 has been pretty much replaced by the AA-11 Archer, which has even more maneuverability and range— plus the ability to engage targets head on. Rather than using engine exhaust, its

seeker can sense the heat signature of a target just from the friction of air passing over the airframe. The design is similar to that of the American AIM-9 Sidewinder, but with more speed and agility. The increase in agility is the result of several sets of control surfaces on the nose, the tail, and in the exhaust path of the missile, enabling it to pull turns much harder than any manned aircraft. But when a target gets inside IR range, there is still the need for a gun. On the MiG it's a GSh-301 30mm cannon, which Mikoyan maintains will reliably destroy target aircraft (within parameters) with five rounds. During development of the aircraft, Mikhail Waldenberg was concerned that the magazine wouldn't hold enough ammunition, but during initial trials, the gun refused to fire

A ground crewman loads air-to-ground rockets into a rocket pod. These missiles are of the type used on the MiG-29.

bursts longer than five rounds because it jammed. This was naturally worrisome to Waldenberg until they considered that the drone aircraft were coming unglued anyway. Further tests revealed that the whole system was spectacularly accurate and that the magazine capacity was far more generous than would ever be needed. Mikoyan claims the gun is the lightest of its type in any fighter, which may explain why it also has an extremely short barrel life, only 2,000 rounds.

Weapons on a fighter aircraft are only as good as the detection and designation system. On modern aircraft, these systems comprise a very large percentage of the fighter's weight, bulk, and cost. All contemporary fighters incorporate radar and computers, both of which are re-

quired for most engagements. What makes the MiG and its sibling, the Sukhoi-27, special in comparison is the integration of weapons, computers, and sensors with the pilot's helmet-mounted sight to form a seamless web of offensive and defensive capabilities. The example Waldenberg likes to cite is: Imagine you're engaging a target at high altitude, over the clouds. The enemy runs from you at long range, dives for the clouds; you can track him while remaining undetected because the IRST detects him passively. The IRST is computer-linked to the fire-control system, the HUD, the missile seekers, and the radar. When you chase your target this way, he has no warning of your approach unless he can see you or is warned by another aircraft or ground control. If he is

A garden-variety MiG-29A takes the active.

The MiG-29C's fuselage just aft of the cockpit offers the only obvious clue to its identity, a slight bulge that allegedly accommodates extra fuel and avionics. Mikoyan doesn't consider this model a major modification of the type (as the F-15E is, for example, when compared to the earlier models).

Tucked into its dispersal parking spot a Fulcrum awaits the call to arms.

Despite an extra-long proboscis, the Fulcrum K fits the elevator on the carrier Kuznetzov *(formerly called the* Tbilisi). *This picture was* made during initial carrier trials and shows the first navalized prototype, number 311. via Jon Lake/World Air Power Journal

A MiG-29K lands aboard the Kuznetzov. via Jon Lake/*World Air Power Journal*

warned, he will dive into the clouds to escape. The IRST doesn't work in clouds, but the radar does, so it automatically transmits when the IR sensor loses its lock on the target. The HUD continues to display the target symbology and the data for target engagement; the target's radar-warning receiver will light up and provide a warning. As the target breaks out of the clouds, the radar immediately reverts to stand-by and the IRST takes over again. The weapon appropriate for the tactical situation can be selected and its firing solution will be displayed on the HUD; for distant targets, it will be a missile, and for closer ones, it will be the cannon. If the cannon is selected, a laser rangefinder will energize, precisely measuring the distance and tracking angle to the target, far more accurately than radar. This data is automatically processed by the computers and displayed in the HUD. If the pilot slaves the cannon to the fire-control computer, the weapon will automatically fire when a solution is achieved.

With missiles, the pilot listens for the lock-on tone, indicating a solution, and then uses the trigger on the control column to launch a missile.

More than 800 MiG-29s have been built and serve with many air forces in Europe and Asia. The Commonwealth of Independent States Air Force maintains about 500 with Frontal aviation units throughout the various republics of what used to be the Soviet Union. Most are the A model, the version described throughout this book.

Fulcrum B

But there is also a two-seat trainer model, designated MiG-29UB (or Fulcrum B, to NATO), of which there are eighty or more. The B model is an interesting variant and the only one that the Russians have allowed any Western pilot to fly (although the former East German single-seaters have been thoroughly checked out by West German and American pilots since unification). It lacks radar but retains the IRST system. The back seat

normally accommodates an instructor-pilot when the aircraft is being used to train operational pilots; the back-seater has a periscope that can be extended and retracted, providing limited forward visibility. It's possible to land and take off with the periscope extended, but not much more.

Only Canadian Air Force pilot Major Bob Wade has been able to fly the B model from the front seat, although others have been offered the chance. His 12min flight in 1989 provided many insights into the MiG's character and capabilities, but didn't include everything; the HUD and IRST were both left off, so these major systems remain somewhat shrouded in secrecy. Although a disappointment to Western analysts, this wasn't a surprise; such secrecy is pretty much standard procedure for all air forces. (Even the old USAF F-4G Wild Weasel's APR-47, now retired from active duty, is seldom photographed and never turned on.)

Although the B model lacks radar, and with it any long-range, tactical air-to-air capability, the IRST and fire controls, the laser rangefinder, and weapons re-

German MiG with a start cart ready to assist with the preliminaries. The German Air Force acquired twenty single-seat MiG-29s and four UB trainers after reunification. All are being incorporated in a new wing that will include Fulcrums and F-4 Phantoms. Jon Lake/*World Air Power Journal*

As almost anywhere else, the squadron commander's airplane gets the extra bells and whistles. This one belongs to Oberst Manfred Menge of Jagdfliegergeschwader (commonly called JDG) 3. The Germans have repainted all the MiGs in their standard gray camouflage pattern but have retained the insignia of JDG 3. Jon Lake/World Air Power Journal

quired for ground attack missions are functional. And the back-seater can call up bogus bogies on the IRST and HUD, simulate engine fires and other disasters on the warning panel, and provide other cues to the poor pilot being trained.

Fulcrum C

A slightly modified MiG-29, now designated by NATO as the Fulcrum C, started appearing in 1989. Mikoyan doesn't consider this a new model but an extension of the existing design. The aircraft is notable for its larger dorsal area, with a small hump directly astern of the cockpit, housing additional fuel and electronics components. The improved model has been incorporated into squadrons and seems to be used without distinction.

Fulcrum K

In 1980, the then-Soviet Union decided to begin building an aircraft carrier as part of a new vision of the Soviet Navy designed by Admiral Gorshkov. Until then, the Russian fleet operated helicopters and Yak-38 jump jets from small *Kiev*-class carriers. The new carrier, originally called the *Tbilisi* but now the *Admiral Nikolay Kuznetsov*, was designed to accommodate far more capable fighters than the Yak-38 (an extremely dangerous design, with short range and limited offensive capability). Therefore, both Mikoyan and Sukhoi Design Bureaus began developing aircraft for carrier-based operations.

The MiG-29 version is designated the K model for *korabelny*, the Russian word for "naval." It dispenses with the special intake doors in favor of stronger landing gear, a tail hook, folding wings, a redesigned stabilator, and a modified IRST system and air refueling capability. The fire-control system is improved, and the IRST may (they aren't telling) provide an IR imaging system like the FLIR on West-

Access panels removed, a German Fulcrum undergoes routine maintenance. Jon Lake/ *World Air Power Journal*

ern aircraft, providing enhanced night ground attack capability.

Besides the Russian carrier requirement, a likely customer for a navalized fighter would be India. The Indians have been buying MiG-29s for years and like them very much. They've also recently purchased an old aircraft carrier from Britain for which the Fulcrum would be a natural candidate.

Fulcrum M

The MiG-29 M version is reported by Jon Lake in *World Air Power Journal* to

A German MiG-29 about to touch down on a rain-soaked runway. Jon Lake/*World Air Power Journal*

India has been a long-time customer for Soviet and Russian military hardware, and an enthusiastic fan of the Fulcrum. This one belongs to No. 47 Squadron, based at Poona, not far from Dehli. Seventy were purchased, the first fifty reportedly for less than $10 million each. via Jon Lake/World Air Power Journal

be a technology demonstrator with four-channel FBW flight controls and multi-function displays like those on the F-15E and F/A-18.

Mikoyan believes the airframe's design is so good that it can be developed far into the future with better engines, flight controls, and avionics.

MiGs old and new: a Czechoslovakian MiG-29 flies with a specially painted MiG-21. Jon Lake/World Air Power Journal

Note the "zappers" and signatures on the side of the engine intake on the MiG-29 in the *foreground.* British Aerospace via Jon Lake/ *World Air Power Journal*

This photo of a MiG-29 in totally clean configuration emphasizes its graceful lines.

Index